RICHARD M. FOXX
NATHAN H. AZRIN

Toilet Training Persons with Developmental Disabilities

A Rapid Program for Day and Nighttime Independent Toileting

Research Press
2612 North Mattis Avenue
Champaign, Illinois 61821

ISBN 0−87822−025−9

Publisher's note to 13th printing, 1993

Since the publication of this book in 1973, most of the toilet training apparatuses used in this program no longer are being manufactured. However, the toilet training procedures can still be implemented without these apparatuses. For toilet training with individual clients, follow the procedures for home training discussed on page 96. For group training, blue litmus paper can be substituted for the urine alert and pants alarm as discussed on page 31. The wet-bed alarm currently is available from J.C. Penney.

Toilet Training Persons with Developmental Disabilities was originally published under the title *Toilet Training the Retarded*.

CONTENTS

TABLES

---

* These Tables are also program forms.

FIGURES

* These Figures are also program forms.

ABOUT THE TOILET TRAINING PROGRAM

The program includes this manual and the program forms, which are replications of some of the tables and figures and the two self-tests in the manual. These forms readily provide information and records necessary for conducting the toilet training program. The tables and figures which appear as program forms are indicated by an asterisk.

PREFACE

The procedures described in this manual have been used to train self-initiated toileting to over 1000 retardates and nonretardates in over 50 different institutions. The manual has been pre-tested by using it as the sole means of instruction for several trainers, and has undergone continuous revision on the basis of their solicited feedback. As a result of their comments, detailed step-by-step descriptions of key techniques along with general statements of strategy and overall rationale have been included.

The audience for this manual are program directors, special educators, ward supervisors and attendants, hospital administrators, and parents of the retarded. Although the procedure is based on learning theory, no technical language is used. The procedures have been formally evaluated in the studies listed in the Reference Section.

The development of the toilet training program has been a gratifying experience. The long-term objective is to develop educational procedures that will elevate the retarded to a more normal level of functioning. In this one area of self-care, we feel that we have succeeded in providing a model for further efforts. We believe that the retardate's mastery of self-toileting will inspire his parents and guardians to attempt similar mastery in other areas. We hope that other psychologists will devise educational techniques for the development of additional skills.

We are indebted to many individuals for their efforts. Peter Levison, Director of Research for the Illinois Department of Mental Health, provided research support for our efforts. R. C. Steck, Superintendent of Anna State Hospital and Wayne Isaacs, Assistant Superintendent, provided the necessary administrative support. Alice Meyer, Orlie Shannon, Jim Stokes, and Ralph Travis supported the development at the program level. As program directors, Nelda Best, Gary Bible, Joe Burnett, Don Haworth, Carol Shepard, David Webster, and Judy Webster implemented the daytime program in the early stages of development. Charles Bugle and Floyd O'Brien assisted in the development of some of the early portions of the daytime program. Tim Sneed assisted greatly in the development of the nighttime program. Individual trainers who assisted in the development of the program are Carolyn Bridges, Rodney Clutts,

John Crider, Afton Jarvis, Glen Lingle, Larry Payne, Rich Patterson, and Fran Simmerman. Special thanks are due Bob Belcher, Curt Carraker, and Ernest Martin for their suggestions and assistance as trainers. Valuable comments and feedback were provided by trainers at other institutions in Illinois including Elgin State Hospital, Lincoln State School, Murray Zone Center, and Tinley Park Mental Health Center. The project was supported in part by Grant #17981 from the National Institute of Mental Health.

We wish to thank the *Journal of Applied Behavior Analysis* for permission to use the picture illustrating the urine alert. Portions of Chapter 2 have appeared previously in *The Journal of Research and Training*, Vol. 1, No. 1, 1973.

RMF
NHA

PART 1 :: DAYTIME TOILET TRAINING

CHAPTER 1

AN EXAMPLE
OF THE TOILET TRAINING PROGRAM

The following is an account of how a staff member, Paul Bennet, initiated and conducted the toilet training program described in this manual. The account is based on a composite of actual experiences of several different staff members and trainees.

Paul Bennet was the Ward Supervisor on a ward containing 30 profoundly retarded men. He was eager to teach the residents how to help themselves rather than merely provide them with custodial care. Bennet chose to begin with a toilet training program.

Where to Begin

Meeting with the Superintendent

Bennet decided that the best way to guarantee the success of a toilet training program would be to obtain the support of the hospital Superintendent. Although sometimes inaccessible, the Superintendent was regarded by the hospital staff as a reasonable man. Bennet made an appointment to meet with the Superintendent as soon as possible. At their meeting a week later, Bennet told the Superintendent that he wanted to start a toilet training program. The Superintendent seemed interested but wasn't quite sure just how important the problem was. Using his own experiences, Bennet described to him in great detail the large number of problems of hygiene and staff effort that wetting and soiling caused. The Superintendent was convinced by the many examples Bennet provided and promised his total support for a toilet training program. Bennet suggested that the Superintendent send a memorandum to the ward staff urging their cooperation in the effort to eliminate incontinence. Bennet also asked him for $300 from the general program fund so that the necessary training supplies could be purchased. The Superintendent agreed to send the memorandum and to approve the request for funds.

Meeting with the Ward Staff

When Bennet received the memorandum, he posted it in the ward nursing station. After he was sure that everyone had seen the memo, he called a ward staff meeting where he explained to the staff what he hoped they would be able to accomplish together. He then asked for anyone with reservations about the program to speak up. A few people had questions about the program, but the only serious question was that of how much extra work would be involved. They settled the question by agreeing that more work would be needed temporarily while training was going on but in the long run there would be less work once the residents were toilet trained.

Pre-Training Arrangements

Following the staff meeting, the next step was to find out just how bad the problem of wetting and soiling was on the ward. Bennet did so by having the attendants check the residents' pants every hour for 3 days. They recorded whether the pants were wet or dry. He also ordered 3 apparatuses that fit into ward toilet bowls to signal correct toiletings and 3 apparatuses that the residents would wear to signal accidents. A few days after the records had been taken, the signaling apparatuses arrived. Now the training could be scheduled. Bennet decided to train the first residents himself. After reading a description of the training procedure several times, Bennet scheduled the training for the following day.

First Training Day

About 7:30 on the first morning, Bennet gathered up the training materials and took them to one of the ward's bathrooms. In the bathroom he placed the training materials: pitchers of coffee, Kool-Aid, and iced cola, several bowls of different candies and chips, the signaling apparatuses, a small pocket timer, individually marked drinking cups, a recording form, and several pairs of underwear. Since 7:00 that morning, the ward staff had been instructed to give fluids to the resident who was to be trained.

Bennet had selected Hal to be the first person trained because Hal was the highest functioning resident on the ward. The pre-training records had shown that Hal was averaging about 6 accidents per day. Hal was 46 years old and had lived in the hospital for 42 of the 46 years. The cause of his retardation was unknown but thought to have resulted from some form of birth trauma. He was thin and partially blind in one eye and had a bad case of cradle cap that went all the way down to his eyebrows. Generally, Hal would cooperate with the staff whenever they attempted to have him do something. There were occasions, however, when he resisted their attempts to work with him. This resistance usually began with a tantrum in which he shouted loudly, followed by a passive resistance phase when he would throw himself on the floor and refuse to move. If the attendants were firm, however, Hal usually ceased his tantrum. Hal's major problem was that he soiled himself. Indeed, Hal seemed to wet his pants "on purpose," for he wet them only when a staff member was standing close to him. He had two other little "tricks" that he especially liked to perform in front of visitors. One was to masturbate whenever a visitor looked at him; the other was to push himself between two people who were talking and then press his face up very close to one of their faces. Bennet felt that Hal "acted up" to gain attention.

To ensure privacy, Bennet asked the staff to have the other residents use the other ward toilet. He also asked the staff to stay away from the training area unless they were needed. When Bennet brought two chairs into the bathroom, one for each of them, he realized that he and Hal would get to know each other very well, since they would be spending 8 hours a day together. Bennet reminded the staff to bring Hal's lunch to the bathroom during lunch time, so that it could be used as rewards during the afternoon.

Bennet had Hal dress in the special underwear he would wear during the training. Two clothing snaps for detecting moisture had been placed in the crotch area of the underpants. In teaching Hal to pull up the underwear, Bennet guided him by putting his hands on top of Hal's hands. As Hal began to raise his pants by himself, Bennet reduced the guidance by lifting his hands off Hal's hands. Bennet continued to keep his hands near Hal's so that he could guide them again if necessary. Bennet praised Hal for any little independent movement as well as praising him when the pants were pulled up. When Hal had the underpants on, Bennet pinned the small pants alarm to the back of the underpants and connected the two wires from the pants alarm to the two snaps in the front of the underpants. Bennet then had Hal sit down on his chair.

Bennet gave Hal three cups of coffee, his favorite drink. After Hal was finished drinking, Bennet placed the urine alert (a plastic signaling bowl) into the toilet bowl. Then Bennet walked over to Hal. He pointed toward the toilet bowl directly across from Hal's chair, lightly touched him on the shoulder, and said, "Hal, go to the toilet." Hal arose from his chair but did not begin walking. Bennet grasped Hal's shirt lightly and guided him toward the toilet. As Hal began walking, Bennet released his grip on the shirt. Hal got to the toilet after two steps, since his chair was only about three feet away. Bennet then pointed at Hal's pants and said, "Pants down." Hal seemed to understand for he grasped the waistband of his pants and pulled them down about three inches. When he stopped, Bennet placed his hands on top of Hal's and gently guided them in lowering the pants. As Bennet had done earlier in teaching Hal to raise his pants, he reduced the guidance as Hal began lowering his pants himself. He then told Hal to sit down on the toilet while pointing at it. Hal sat down by himself without the need for guidance. Bennet turned and set the timer for 20 minutes since Hal had to sit there for 20 minutes or until he used the toilet. Bennet then sat down and waited for Hal to urinate or for 20 minutes to elapse.

After Hal had been sitting on the toilet about 15 minutes, the urine alert sounded, signaling that Hal had urinated in the toilet. To show his delight, Bennet ran over to Hal and excitedly told him, "That's good, Hal, you used the toilet." He hugged Hal and continued to tell him how happy he was that Hal had urinated in the toilet. He waited for Hal to finish urinating and then gave him a large piece of a candy bar which he took from the apron he was wearing. Then he prompted Hal to stand up by touching him lightly on his shoulder. When Hal was standing, Bennet told him to pull his pants up and guided Hal's hands as much as was needed. Hal was doing better. Bennet had only to use his thumb and index finger to guide Hal this time. Then, he took Hal's hand and guided it toward the flush handle after telling Hal to flush the toilet and pointing to the handle. Again Hal needed guidance, but as soon as Bennet could feel that Hal was beginning to push down on the handle,

Bennet lifted his hand from Hal's hand and Hal flushed it himself. Hal smiled and chuckled to himself as if he enjoyed the sound of the flushing toilet. Bennet then disconnected the urine alert and emptied its contents into the toilet. Bennet then directed Hal back to his chair by pointing to the chair and saying, "Hal, sit down." Hal seemed to understand and required no guidance. He walked back to his chair and sat down readily. Bennet then flushed the toilet a second time. Bennet took a cloth, wiped the signaling bowl dry, and reconnected it so it would be ready to signal the next time that Hal urinated in the toilet.

After reinserting the bowl into the toilet, Bennet reset the timer so it would ring 10 minutes later to remind him to begin giving the drinks again. Bennet would now begin teaching Hal how important it was to have dry clothing. He walked over to Hal and asked him if his pants were dry. When Hal made no response, Bennet guided Hal's hand to the crotch of his pants so that Hal was touching his pants. He held an M&M candy close to Hal's mouth and said, "Hal, you're a good fellow, you have dry pants," and placed the M&M in Hal's mouth. Five minutes later, Bennet repeated this procedure of rewarding Hal for having dry pants. During the period that Hal was sitting on the chair, Bennet talked to him continually about how pleased he was that Hal had dry pants.

Exactly 30 minutes after Hal had first been given drinks, the timer rang and he was again offered coffee which he again drank readily. After Hal had drunk several cups of coffee, Bennet prompted him to go to the toilet. This time he just said the word "toilet" and consciously tried not to use as much effort in guiding Hal's hands to pull his pants down. He continued to praise Hal whenever he began any movements by himself. Ten minutes after sitting down, Hal's urine alert sounded, signaling that he had urinated in the toilet a second time. Bennet rushed over, praised and hugged him, and rewarded him again with a large piece of candy. Bennet decided not to tell Hal to stand up but instead just swung his head toward Hal's chair when he was sure that Hal was looking at him. When Hal saw Bennet turn his head toward the chair, he stood up and began raising his pants. Bennet was pleased that Hal had learned to stand up after a simple gesture without the need for direct instruction. And better yet, Hal had learned to raise his pants immediately after arising with no instructions at all.

Since Hal was learning to react to simple gestures, Bennet decided to omit the direct instruction to Hal to flush the toilet. Instead he merely pointed to the flush handle. Again Hal reacted to the gesture; he bent over and flushed it entirely by himself with no need for guidance even though Bennet kept his hand within an inch of Hal's in case Hal needed help. After flushing the toilet, Hal sat down in his chair. Five minutes later, Bennet was rewarding Hal for having dry pants. He continued to check Hal's pants every 5 minutes. Then the timer rang indicating that it was time to give drinks again.

Bennet followed the same sequence every half-hour. He gave Hal drinks, prompted him to the toilet, prompted him to lower his pants and sit down on the toilet, left him on the toilet for 20 minutes or until he voided, and then prompted him to stand up and raise his pants, sent him back to his chair, and then checked his pants every 5 minutes. Each half-hour Bennet reduced the instructions, guidance, and gestures for each skill and could see that Hal was learning to react to very subtle cues.

Two Hours Later

In the past 2 hours Hal had urinated in the toilet during 3 of the 4 half-hour toiletings. However, he had not urinated during the last toileting trial. He had also required more guidance during that last trial, which was an indication that he was beginning to "test" the training situation. Bennet felt that during the last trial Hal had deliberately refrained from urinating. Since Hal was fidgeting in his chair, Bennet knew that Hal had to urinate. When Bennet motioned for him to go to the toilet, Hal suddenly began shouting loudly and slumped to the floor. Hal had begun to "test" Bennet.

A crucial point in the training program had been reached. Hal was attempting to terminate the training program. Bennet had expected this would occur and knew that he must not let it happen; Hal had to learn that nothing he did would postpone or terminate his learning to toilet himself. Accordingly, Bennet lifted Hal up and grasping his shirt, guided him toward the toilet. As Hal began moving, Bennet stopped guiding him but kept his hand on Hal's shirt in case he stopped moving. When Hal was told to pull his pants down, he refused, despite having done it six times before. Bennet quickly grasped Hal's hands and guided him in lowering his pants. Hal didn't like being guided and began lowering the pants himself. When Bennet pointed to the toilet, Hal refused to sit down. Bennet placed his hand on Hal's shoulder and used just enough guidance to seat Hal on the toilet. A few minutes after sitting down, Hal began to masturbate. Bennet walked over to Hal, called him by name, and handed him a cup in an attempt to distract him. Hal began twirling the cup and stopped masturbating. During this toileting trial, Hal did not urinate. After Hal had spent the allotted 20 minutes on the toilet, Bennet motioned with his head for Hal to stand up. Hal complied readily, pulled his pants up himself, and walked to his chair.

When Hal was seated, Bennet asked him if his pants were dry and had him touch his pants and rewarded him with praise and some candy. Five minutes later, Bennet again inspected Hal's pants. He knew that Hal had to urinate. All he could do was wait to see whether Hal would urinate in the toilet or in his pants. While Hal was sitting on his chair awaiting the next half-hour's toileting, his pants alarm sounded. Hal had had an accident. Now Bennet would teach Hal why he should not wet his pants. Hal had learned the advantages of staying dry; now he must learn the disadvantages of wetting his pants. Hal had soaked his pants and his canvas shoes, and was sitting in a puddle by the time Bennet reached him. Bennet told Hal, "No," when he first heard the alarm sound. Then when he reached Hal's chair, he quickly grasped Hal's shoulders so that they were face to face and said, "No, don't wet your pants." He had oriented Hal so that he could be sure that Hal was listening to him. He disconnected the wires so that the alarm would stop ringing.

Hal would now have to learn to clean up his accidents. Bennet felt certain that Hal would resist any attempts to require him to clean up. As a result, Bennet would use as much guidance as necessary to ensure that Hal completed each act in cleaning up. Whenever possible, of course, he would reduce the guidance as Hal began to clean up by himself. Bennet guided Hal over to the table where he guided him in picking up a cloth. After guiding Hal back to his chair, Bennet guided him in wiping up the puddle of urine. Hal started to back away from the chair, but Bennet quickly stopped him and leaned against him so that he bent forward slightly, making it easier for Bennet to guide Hal. The wiping then continued. After Hal had wiped up the urine, Bennet guided him to the table and told him to place the wet cloth in a bucket under the table. He then guided Hal back to his chair.

Bennet didn't permit Hal to remain seated; instead he told him that he must practice going to the toilet. Bennet would have Hal practice going to the toilet several times. In each trial Hal would be required to practice all of the component steps necessary when toileting. This required practice would teach Hal the acceptable alternative to wetting his pants. Bennet realized that a good deal of guidance would again be necessary since Hal would probably resist Bennet's instructions to practice going to the toilet. Even though he was upset, Bennet kept his voice even, trying to show little emotion as he said, "Hal, practice going to the toilet." Since Hal made no movement toward the toilet, Bennet guided him there rapidly and told him to practice pulling his pants down. When Hal made no attempt to lower his pants, Bennet guided Hal's hands very quickly in lowering his shorts. Hal was then directed to sit on the toilet. After he had been sitting about 10 seconds, Bennet told him to stand up and practice raising his pants. Hal started to raise them but then stopped. As Bennet began guiding Hal's hands, Hal tried to pull them away. Bennet held Hal's hands rigid until he stopped resisting and then began guiding him again. At this point, Hal finished raising the pants himself. Bennet had Hal practice 5 times going back and forth to the toilet, raising and lowering his pants, and sitting on the toilet for just a few seconds. At the end of the fifth practice trial, the timer rang, indicating that the next half-hour's scheduled toileting was to begin. Hal would change into dry pants at the end of the next 20-minute toileting period or after he urinated in the toilet. Bennet would now teach Hal that he could not eat or drink anymore while wearing soiled pants. Hal would learn that he must have dry pants before enjoying food and beverages.

Bennet took a cup of coffee over to Hal who was standing in his wet pants. He said, "Hal, are your pants dry?" Hal said nothing and reached for the coffee. Bennet grasped Hal's outstretched hand and guided it so that Hal was touching his wet pants. Bennet told him, "No, Hal, no coffee for you, you have wet pants." Hal began shouting as he had earlier, but Bennet ignored him and carried the cup back to the table. Bennet repeated the procedure using a piece of candy. He showed Hal the candy, asked if his pants were dry, had Hal feel his pants, and then told him that he could not have candy because his pants were wet. Bennet then prompted Hal to the toilet.

Lunch Time

By lunch time the procedure was being conducted more smoothly. Hal had had only one accident. He was requiring less assistance each time he was sent to the toilet. When Hal's lunch arrived, Bennet used spoon-sized portions as rewards during the 5-minute dry-pants inspections that were occurring whenever Hal was not on the toilet.

2:00 P.M.

By 2:00 Hal had urinated during several more of the half-hour toiletings. He had had another accident at 1:45, but that was to be expected. In fact, it was important that he have one or two accidents during the training since he had to learn what would happen to him when he wet his pants. It was all part of teaching him responsibility for his own toileting behavior. After the second accident, Hal seemed noticeably upset when he had been told, "No, don't wet your pants." He didn't seem to enjoy missing his drinks, cleaning up, or the practice sessions. Hal was learning that Bennet's reactions to accidents were consistent and that wetting himself would no longer be tolerated.

At 2:00 Bennet began offering Hal only one cup of fluid each half-hour. The training would end in another two hours, and Hal had already drunk many cups of fluid. During the last hour of training, he would be offered only a few sips of the drinks every 30 minutes.

4:00 P.M.

At 4:00 the day's training ended. Bennet had spent 8 hours in the toilet with Hal, except for the half-hour he had taken for lunch. During Bennet's lunch time he was relieved by an aide who had watched part of the

9

training that morning. Bennet removed the pants signal and had Hal remove the underwear. Then Bennet had Hal put his trousers back on because he was being sent back to the ward where he usually wore trousers without underpants. Bennet escorted Hal back to the ward, then returned to the bathroom and put the training equipment away. In his office, Bennet went over a record he had kept of the day's events. He was pleased when the record showed that as the day wore on, Hal urinated more quickly after sitting on the toilet. The records also showed that Hal had had only 2 accidents and 11 correct urinations. He had refused to approach the toilet on a couple of occasions, but Bennet had expected Hal to "test" the training situation. What was encouraging was that Hal seemed to enjoy the attention and rewards that he had received. He also had learned many of the skills that he needed to toilet himself. He could pull his pants up and down and understood what "Go to the toilet" meant. Furthermore, he would initiate and complete many of the toileting acts without the need for reminders.

After reviewing the training records, Bennet went to the ward nursing station and met with the evening shift. He told them to watch Hal closely. If they found him in wet pants, they were to require Hal to clean up any puddles and to change his pants himself.

Second Training Day

When Bennet arrived at work the next morning, a staff member jokingly said, "I don't know what you did for Hal, but he is standing down by the toilet as if he's waiting for you." The thought occurred to Bennet that yesterday was probably the most attention that Hal had received in all his years in the institution. A review of a record of accidents that the evening shift had kept showed that Hal had had several accidents the previous night. But Bennet expected this since Hal had not finished his training. Bennet went to his office, obtained the training equipment, and went to the bathroom where Hal was waiting.

When the time came to prompt Hal to the toilet for the first time that day, Bennet began by using the same level of instructions, gestures, and guidance that Hal had been responding to on the last toileting trial of the previous day. Bennet did not want to backtrack unless it was absolutely necessary. By beginning at the same level at which the previous day's training ended, a smooth day-to-day transition would be maintained.

The training day went smoothly. Hal continued to urinate within a few minutes after sitting on the toilet and was approaching the toilet and raising and lowering his pants with more independence. Hal had tried very hard to please; he had 13 correct urinations and had tested only once when he had an accident just before the training day ended.

Third Training Day

During the first 3 hours of the third day, Hal had progressed to the point where he would walk to the toilet whenever Bennet shifted his eyes in that direction. Hal was watching Bennet very closely as if he were trying to figure out when Bennet would look at the toilet. Since Bennet's eyes were always naturally moving about, Hal could never be sure whether or not Bennet was signaling him to go. As a result, Hal would begin toileting himself soon without any conscious prompting on Bennet's part.

At 11:00 Hal arose from his chair with no prompt and went to the toilet by himself. Bennet rushed over to Hal, praising and hugging him. Bennet became overly excited and tried to prompt Hal to stand up before he was finished. Hal sprayed the floor with urine but Bennet directed him to sit on the toilet bowl again until he finished urinating. From now on he would not prompt Hal to the toilet. Hal would have to decide for himself when to go to the toilet. Bennet moved Hal's chair two feet farther back from the toilet so that the next time he went to the toilet he would be walking farther. By moving Hal's chair farther back after each self-initiated toileting, Bennet would eventually have Hal self-initiating from the ward day room where Hal normally spent most of his time. At that point the training would end since Hal would be capable of toileting himself from anywhere on the ward. As soon as Hal returned to his chair, Bennet offered him several cups of fluid. He would now give the fluids after a self-initiation rather than every 30 minutes. Thus, Hal would not regard the fluids as a prompt to toilet himself, since his urge to urinate again would be slight immediately following a urination.

Within a few minutes, Hal self-initiated again. Bennet moved his chair back a few feet farther and gave him several cups of soda. Bennet had changed from coffee to soda, as he had done each day, because Hal had had eight cups of coffee that day and Bennet did not want to upset his stomach. Bennet would now check Hal's pants only every 10 minutes until he self-initiated again, at which time he would check him only every 20 minutes. After each self-initiation, Bennet would lengthen the time between dry-pants inspections. Eventually, he would be checking Hal's pants every 2 hours, the same interval that Hal's pants would be checked after he finished training. When Hal self-initiated the third time, Bennet did not give him a candy reward. He would begin giving Hal candy and drinks for only some of the toiletings, eventually stopping rewards entirely so that Hal would no longer expect rewards for urinating. Thereafter Hal would be rewarded only at the dry-pants inspections.

Hal had self-initiated 2 more times, and his chair had been moved out into the hallway. But 20 minutes later Hal had an accident. From now on, Hal would be required to clean up the general area where the accident occurred, to change into clean clothing, and to practice going to the toilet. This "correction" of the accident was scheduled to last for 30 minutes. Since Hal could now toilet himself, more would be required of him following an accident. When Bennet heard Hal's pants alarm he told Hal, "No, don't wet your pants" and disconnected the pants alarm. Then he guided Hal to the ward cleaning closet, where he guided Hal in filling a pail with water and disinfectant. Bennet also had Hal pick up a mop and carry it and the pail back to the spot where the accident occurred. Five minutes had elapsed since the accident, which meant that Hal had to mop the general area where he had the accident for 10 minutes. When Hal had finished mopping (which he didn't like—Bennet had to guide Hal's hands in the mopping motions several times), Bennet had Hal carry the pail to a sink and empty it. Bennet then escorted Hal back to the closet where he put the mop and pail away. He then guided Hal down the hallway to the ward clothing room. He guided Hal in picking up a clean pair of pants and had him carry them back to the bathroom. Bennet then required Hal to take off his wet pants and to dry himself off with a cloth. Hal was somewhat resistive but began drying himself after

Bennet had guided him a few times. Bennet then required Hal to put on his clean pants and carry his wet pants to the sink where he had to soak them and wring them out. Then Bennet had Hal take his wet pants into the shower room and hang them up to dry. Hal was then required to practice going to the toilet 6 times from the location where he wet his pants. Bennet gave the instructions to practice in an even tone of voice devoid of emotion. Hal then returned to his chair.

After the accident, Hal self-initiated 4 more times which was enough to convince Bennet that Hal was ready for the Maintenance Program. After each self-initiation, Bennet had checked Hal's pants less frequently to the point where he was checking Hal only every 2 hours—the same interval between pants checks as on the Maintenance Program. Bennet escorted Hal back to the ward day room and then met with the ward staff. Bennet would work with the staff for the first few days until they all understood how to conduct the Maintenance Program. Hal's Maintenance Program began as soon as he was returned to the day room.

First Maintenance Day

Bennet spent the entire day conducting the Maintenance Program for Hal. He checked Hal's pants at 6 regularly scheduled checks: mealtimes, bedtime, and two snack periods. He also made several spontaneous checks throughout the day. That morning he checked Hal's pants as he was about to enter the dining room for breakfast. He asked Hal, "Are your pants dry?" Hal nodded that they were and reached down and touched the crotch of his pants. Since Hal's pants were dry, Bennet praised him and then Hal proceeded to the dining room and ate his breakfast without any delay. At 9:30, Bennet checked Hal's pants, asking him if he had dry pants. Since his pants were dry, Bennet praised him and gave him a piece of candy as a snack. At lunch time Bennet found Hal's pants wet as he was about to enter the dining room. He asked Hal if his pants were dry. Hal acted as if he knew he had done something wrong because he refused to look at Bennet. Bennet took Hal's hand and guided it to the wet spot. "Your pants are wet, you must clean up and practice before you eat." Bennet told the dietary staff to hold Hal's food tray. Then he had Hal mop up a puddle near Hal's favorite spot in the day room and change and wash his pants. Hal then had to practice going to the toilet 6 times from different locations on the ward. The mopping, clothes changing, and practice took 30 minutes to complete. One hour after the accident was discovered Hal went in the dining room to eat his lunch. Bennet checked Hal at the 2:30 snack period, asked if his pants were dry, and was pleased that he was dry. He gave Hal a snack and praise. Bennet remained on the ward until Hal had gone to bed. He had the staff watch him check Hal before supper and bedtime so they would see how the dry-pants inspections should be made.

Second Maintenance Day

Hal was found wet that morning at the 9:30 snack period. Bennet showed him the snack and told him he could not have it because his pants were wet. He then had Hal mop the area where he had wet and change and wash his clothing until 30 minutes had passed since he was found wet. Bennet then had Hal practice going to the toilet from several locations on the ward. Hal kept his pants dry the rest of the day. Bennet had several of the staff conduct the dry-pants checks while he watched them. He also had them take over the Cleanliness Training following Hal's accident at 9:30, so that they could learn how to give the guidance and instructions.

Third Maintenance Day

Hal stayed dry all day. Bennet showed more of the staff how to make the Maintenance checks. By day's end most of the staff had been trained in carrying out the Maintenance procedure. Bennet decided to wait a few days before attempting to train another resident in order to give the ward staff sufficient opportunity to conduct the Maintenance Program by themselves. The postponement would also allow him to be available to help the staff if they had any questions.

Fourth Maintenance Day

Bennet continued to watch various staff members conduct the dry-pants checks throughout the day. Hal had one accident just before bedtime. His bedtime was postponed for one hour until he had cleaned up, changed his clothes, and practiced. Several of the staff took turns working with Hal during the required cleaning up and practice. During that period Bennet remained in the background, commenting only if the procedures were being conducted improperly.

In the past few days, Bennet noticed that Hal had stopped masturbating around visitors and attempting to distract their conversations, possibly because he was receiving so much attention for keeping his pants dry. Apparently Hal had learned to gain attention for remaining dry as a substitute for seeking attention through obnoxious behaviors.

Fifth Maintenance Day

The staff was now running the Maintenance themselves. For each work shift, Bennet appointed a Maintenance Supervisor who was responsible for checking Hal's pants during that shift. The Training and Maintenance Programs were working out well and Bennet was eager to start training more residents within a few days. He also made a point of informing the Superintendent of the initial success of the program. Hal was dry all day. Forty-six years of wetting and soiling had come to an end.

Chapter 2

OVERVIEW OF THE
TOILET TRAINING PROGRAM

The Plight of the
Profoundly and Severely Retarded

Retardation is a major problem affecting about seven million Americans, four percent of the population. The IQ test score of 70 is considered the dividing line below which one is considered retarded. A person having an IQ of 60-70 appears dull and slow to learn but otherwise he seems similar to higher IQ persons in that he cares for himself, carries on conversation, appears conscious of his appearance, and interacts socially. As the IQ score decreases, however, changes occur in addition to a decreased learning ability. At IQ scores below 20, the individual does not converse. Indeed, he probably has never uttered a word. If his clothes are untidy, he seems unaware of it. He spends much of his time stimulating himself such as endlessly rocking back and forth when seated. In addition to his intellectual deficit, he is likely to have serious physical debilities, such as severe hearing loss, partial blindness, paralysis or spasticity of an arm, leg, or hand. Consequently, he is not likely to have normal sensory input or normal manipulative or locomotive abilities. These physical deficits contribute to his apparent intellectual deficit and cause him to appear generally inattentive to the actions of others and unwilling to learn. He is formally classified as severely or profoundly retarded, as are over 300,000 other retardates of similar deficit. So incapable of independent functioning, he will almost certainly be placed in an institution.

Training Programs
for the Untrainable Retarded

The profoundly retarded rarely receive the benefits of training programs. Retardates with IQ scores of 40 or greater are characterized as mildly or moderately retarded and often are given formal classes. If, however, they have IQ scores below 40, they are classified as "untrainable" and little seems to be gained by attempting to train them. The younger profoundly retarded are more fortunate for our traditions dictate that children should be educated. Current concern for the retarded has caused a gratifying increase in educational programs, especially within public schools. Since the "untrainable" retardate is usually ineligible for these classes, he does not benefit from this very recent and enlightened concern. If he is in an institution, he has a chance of receiving attention and training while still young. Volunteers are relatively eager to play with and teach the helpless and needy child. When he matures, however, these community volunteers are not likely to return for a second visit. His cuteness and promise are gone even though his need and helplessness continue. The most dedicated institutional staff are likely to share this feeling of futility, having tried and failed in the past to overcome the barriers presented by deficits in intelligence, communication, attention, sensory input, and motor skills. The untrainable classification seems justified and if he is an adult the urge is slight to attempt what seems to be the impossible.

Toileting by the Untrainable Retarded

Failure of the low functioning retarded to toilet themselves greatly contributes to the opinion that they are untrainable. Almost all normal children are toilet trained by about three years of age and almost certainly by school age. The sight of a mature adult still soiling himself is a marked deviation from the norm. The odor and filth accompanying this incontinence repels any sympathetic attempts to interact with him. He is located on a ward with more than 30 other profoundly retarded residents, all of whom are totally incontinent. The entire crotch area of his pants is stained by a recent urination and a puddle remains at his feet since he has not moved away. He has been in the institution since early childhood when his parents were unable to continuously care for him at home. They attempted to toilet train him with patience, sympathy, and love as have several institutional staff members. When asked why he did not go to the toilet, he does not answer since he does not speak. Indeed, he did not respond to the question, perhaps because of inattentiveness or his partial hearing loss that prevents him from hearing the inquiry. He had been taken to the toilet only half an hour earlier as part of a special program of scheduled toileting and had enjoyed this special bit of attention from the staff. Although he was seated on the toilet bowl for ten minutes, he did not void his bladder at that time. Now that he has soiled his clothing and the floor, an attendant notices the puddle. As the resident stands passively by, the attendant goes to the clothing room for fresh clothing and to the closet for a mop, returns to the resident, and changes his clothing. While the attendant cleans the floor, the resident is taken by another attendant to the toilet to sit on the toilet bowl for an extended period as a preventative measure. Although the attendants are disturbed by this accident, the resident has welcomed this attention and interaction. Even though he is now seated on the toilet stool for one-half hour, he will soil himself again before the afternoon has passed and the scene will be repeated. If not for these accidents, no one interacts with him except to take him to meals.

The Problem of Incontinence

Incontinence has been one of the major unsolved problems in the care of the institutionalized retarded. Institutional staff spend a great deal of time each day attending to the toileting needs of incontinent retardates. Typically, this care does not represent an educational attempt but seeks only to maintain the resident's health and physical well-being. Some institutional facilities have established toilet training programs in which the residents are taken to the toilet at regularly scheduled periods and rewarded for voiding. This training, if carried out consistently, bladder trains or habit trains the residents, i.e., the resident voids when placed on or led to the toilet but does not initiate his own toileting. Whether the resident remains continent depends primarily on the staff's diligence in adhering to a regularly scheduled program. A habit training program, no matter how successful, has limitations. It decreases the number of training and educational activities that can be scheduled daily since much of the staff's time is occupied in taking residents to and from the toilet. This passive shepherding of residents to the toilets fosters a dependent attitude by the residents and hinders efforts to motivate independence in other areas of their functioning. If incontinence persists, the availability of feces often leads to smearing or coprophagy, a behavioral disorder consisting of the habitual ingestion of feces. Epidemics of intestinal infections or viruses, such as shigella, accompanied by diarrhea, will be common and frequent. Laundry, clothing supplies, sanitation, and cleaning activities will become the staff's dominant concern rather than the education of the resident. Family visits will be discouraged, community concern will arise regarding this "snakepit," and staff interaction with the residents will decrease to the minimum possible.

Existing Training Procedures: Recent Progress

Within the past ten years, training procedures based upon behavior modification have offered hope for raising the level of functioning of the retarded. Using principles of learning, this learning therapy approach has been responsible for the token economy for motivating mental hospital patients, programmed instruction now widely used in public schools, and treatment of several other problem areas where individuals suffer from learning and motivational deficits.

The learning therapy approach shows that even the very profoundly retarded adult resident can be toilet trained by using procedures that optimize the learning process. Basically, all the procedures stress the importance of rewarding correct toileting, dealing with the toileting act one small step at a time, rewarding immediately and consistently, and eliminating unintended rewards (attention) for accidents. Although some problems still remain, such as the long period of several weeks required for training, limited success with some residents, and frequent relapse, the major thrust of these combined efforts of many investigators is unequivocal—this intensive learning approach has succeeded in toilet training whereas previous methods have not.

How Much Training Is Trained?
Our Objective

Toilet training is sometimes interpreted to mean only that the resident learns to void himself when he is seated on the toilet bowl. The objective of this manual is greater in scope. The goal is not merely to keep the ward clean of excrement, but to elevate the retarded to the highest level of functioning possible by training self-initiated toileting. Thus, the common practice of leading the passive resident to the toilet every hour is not a solution, but a demonstration, of the problem of accepting the retarded resident's helpless and dependent state. The objective of this manual is that the resident be motivated to toilet himself on his own initiative without prompting of any sort, become sensitive to his appearance, and perform all of the necessary steps of undressing and dressing without assistance. From this perspective, the goal is not to train a bladder sphincter muscle to relax or contract on command but to educate a person to function independently and with social awareness.

Rationale of the Toilet Training Program

The rationale used in developing this toilet training program is that the process involved in toileting is not simply a matter of responding to bladder and bowel pressures, but rather is a complex social process. Normal individuals toilet themselves to avoid the embarrassment of having an accident. We do not wait until pressure from our bladder or bowels is uncomfortable before going to the toilet. Rather, the slightest pressure will prompt us to go to the toilet. Examples of this occur every day. People toilet themselves before going to someone's house for a social occasion. Or, a person typically attempts to urinate before a meeting which may last several hours, and thus avoid the embarrassment of having to interrupt the meeting. People feel more comfortable in their own bathrooms and will go to extremes to toilet there before leaving their homes. So we see that correct toileting behavior is really supported by the desire to avoid unpleasant social reactions rather than a reliance on bladder pressure to prompt us to the toilet. Given this rationale, the toileting program focuses on the appearance of the resident's clothing rather than on whether he has toileted himself.

Some ward staff have mistakenly taught residents to respond only to bladder or bowel pressure. As a result, these residents continue to have occasional accidents since they have been taught to wait until the pressure on their bladder or bowels is demanding before going to the toilet. Waiting until the last moment before seeking the bathroom increases the chances that the resident will have an accident before he can lower his pants. The present procedure, however, teaches the individual to regularly toilet himself when only minimal bladder pressure is present. The resident learns to keep his pants clean and dry by frequently toileting himself and thereby reduces the number of accidents he will have. Readers who have children may remember when their child, although toilet trained for several years, had an accident in his pants. When asked why, the child usually said that he had been playing and was too busy to go to the bathroom. He had waited until the bladder pressure was so intense that when he reached the bathroom, he relaxed his sphincter before reaching the toilet stool. The present toilet training program avoids this problem since the resident will have a long history of toileting himself when only minimal bladder pressure is present.

Training Strategy

The overall strategy is a reward and systems approach in which all phases of the ward environment affecting continence are changed in the direction needed to produce total continence. The components of this strategy are:

Correct vs. Incorrect Response
The resident learns the *correct response* of voiding himself quickly when seated on the toilet, but not to void at all in his clothing, the *incorrect response*.

Learning vs. Motivation
The resident first learns how to toilet himself but then motivation is provided so that he will want to continue using this new skill.

Rewards

Rewards, events which are highly desired by the resident, are used to provide strong motivation during and after learning.

Multiple Rewards

Since a reward can adapt out, i.e., the recipient can become sated, several different types of rewards are used concurrently.

Immediate Reward

Learning is most rapid when the reward is given immediately for the correct performance. Therefore, a method of immediate detection of urination is used.

Association of Reward with Response

Conditioning principles state that the reward should be closely associated with the correct response but be absent when no response is made. With each act of elimination while seated on the toilet paired with a reward, the act of sitting on the toilet seat will create the desire to eliminate.

Number of Trials

Learning is most rapid when many trials are given. Since urination normally occurs only a few times each day, the natural frequency of urination is increased to provide more frequent opportunities to learn.

Imitation

Learning is facilitated by observing others perform the task correctly. Consequently, training is conducted with two or more residents at one time.

Incompatible Responses

Actions that are incompatible or interfere with toileting, such as reluctance to leave a comfortable chair or to walk a long distance to the toilet are reduced.

Toileting Without Being Prompted

Prompting is initially needed in training, but must be eliminated or "faded out" some time thereafter. A fading procedure is used to achieve independent toileting.

Inhibition of Accidents

According to learning principles, a misbehavior can be eliminated effectively when it consistently and immediately results in some negative reaction. Since the institutionalized retarded already have a very low level of satisfaction, a special type of negative reaction to the accidents is used.

Immediate Reaction to Accidents

As is true of rewarding correct toileting, a method is used for immediately detecting the act of soiling.

Associated Motor Skills

All motor skills that are prerequisite to voiding are taught, such as walking to the toilet, dressing and undressing properly, and flushing the toilet immediately after elimination.

Staff Supervision and Motivation

Since the ward staff are the agents for motivating the resident to remain continent long after training is completed, a system of supervising and motivating staff members is used.

How Long Does It Take to Train the Residents?

An experienced trainer can completely train a resident to toilet himself independently in four days. This is an average figure; the speed with which a specific resident is trained is influenced by many factors. For example, if the resident can already dress himself and follow instructions, training is usually accomplished within one or two days. If the resident is a major behavioral problem and has many physical limitations, training could require two weeks or more. Another factor is the resident's level of functioning as measured by the IQ score. The higher the IQ, the more rapidly the resident will be trained, although a paradoxical reversal sometimes occurs in that the higher IQ resident can be more resourceful in resisting training if he so chooses. The skill of the trainers is certainly another factor. The more training the trainers do, the more proficient they become. Training the first residents usually takes much longer than for subsequent trainees.

Who Can Be Trained?

Physical incapabilities will exclude some residents from the program. Since the purpose of the training is to teach self-initiated toileting, the resident must have the following physical capabilities:

1. He must be *ambulatory* so that he can walk to the toilet by himself from any place on the ward.

2. He must have *some motor control of his hands* since he will have to pull his pants up and down to toilet.

3. He must have *some sight* so that he can find his way to the toilet.

4. He must have a *minimum of receptive language*, i.e., an understanding of the very simplest commands. Residents often do not

respond to simple commands because they are unmotivated, not because they do not understand. Unresponsiveness is generally not a problem in the toilet training program since there are sufficient incentives to motivate the resident to comply with the trainer's requests.

Deafness is not a problem since gestural rather than verbal prompts can be used to toilet train the deaf resident. Age is generally not a restriction. Prospective candidates for toilet training are persons over the age of two-and-one-half; at the other extreme, retardates as old as seventy-two have been successfully trained.

      If a resident is ambulatory, has motor control, has at least partial sight, and responds to simple commands, he is trainable unless he has a medical problem.

CHAPTER 3

PREPARATION FOR TOILET TRAINING

Medical Examination Before Training

Before beginning the training program, the residents should have a thorough physical examination. When a resident proves difficult to train, a medical examination may reveal a physical problem that prevents voluntary control of the bladder or bowels. For example, a prolapsed rectum makes it impossible for the resident to control his bowel movements. Corrective surgery can usually eliminate this condition. A prior medical examination would have revealed this problem. During training, residents may seem to warrant a more thorough urogenital examination even though they have had a general physical examination. For example, if a resident dribbles in his pants continuously, rather than voiding a large volume at one time, physical problems should be suspected. Neurological impairment can also cause incontinence. This is especially true for the brain-damaged patient. For these patients, it is especially important that they receive not only a general physical checkup but also a neurological examination. Before beginning the training program, thoroughly review the residents' medical records. A resident may be diabetic and thereby require the use of artificially sweetened candies and fluids during the training program. Or, a resident may be allergic to some of the treats, such as chocolate, used for rewards. If a resident has a history of seizures, he should be given a kidney function test prior to beginning training.

Recording Prior to Training

It is important to determine the frequency of each resident's incontinence prior to training because it provides an objective means of evaluating the seriousness of the incontinence problem and the need for the training program. Figure 1 shows the Pre-Training Accident Record used for this purpose. The trainers or ward staff check the pants of all residents each hour during an 8-hour period, or longer if possible. At each hourly check, the trainer records either a

Figure 1   Pre-Training Accident Record*

W = Wet
D = Dry

Ward _1_
Date _2/14/73_

Resident's Name	1	2	3	4	5	6	7	8	9	10	11	12	Total Wets
Jimmie T.	W	D	D	D	W	D	D	W	W	D	W	D	5
Billy G.	D	D	W	D	W W	D	D	D	W	D	D	W	5
Eddie P.	D	D	D	D	W	D	D	W	D	W	W	D	4
David K.	D	D	W	W	W	W	D	W	D	D	D	W	6
Sam T.	W	D	W W	D	W W	D	W	D	W W	D	W	D	9
John B.	W	D	D	D	W	D	D	D	W	D	W	D	4
George A.	D	W	W	D	D	W	D	W W	D	D	D	W	6
Bruce Y.	W	W	W	W	D	W	D	D	W	W W	D	W	9
Carl D.	D	D	W	W	W	W	W	D	W	D	D	W	7
Ronnie G.	D	D	W	D	W W	D	D	D	W W	W	D	D	6

Checked by _____ a Smith

W (Wet) or D (Dry) in the appropriate block. If the pants are wet, they are changed so that any wetting during the next hour is not confused with a previous wetting. Any accidents occurring between the hourly checks are also recorded if detected and the pants changed. Thus, there could be 2 W's recorded under the same hour.

26

Since the number of accidents may vary from day to day, you should record for a minimum of 3 days. The records can then be transformed into the average number of accidents per day. For example, a resident observed to be wet 5, 6, and 7 times during the 3 days of observation has an average of 6 accidents per day.

Female residents should be required to wear underpants during this pre-training assessment of accidents as well as during training and immediately after training so as to permit adequate detection of accidents. Otherwise, detection of accidents both prior to and after training may be impossible since female residents can urinate while standing, leaving no traces of wetness on their dresses. The use of underpants overcomes this problem. Some female residents may refuse to wear underpants and remove them at the first opportunity. This problem is solved by frequently rewarding the resident for keeping her underpants on and then gradually stretching out the time between rewards.

Where to Train Residents

Toilet training should be conducted in the same toilet that the resident will be using. Training residents in a different toilet may confuse the resident after the training period, since he may not be able to generalize his learning from one situation to another. Inconvenience may result from utilizing the ward toilet but the long-term benefits justify the inconveniences.

Resident to Trainer Ratio

The ideal resident to trainer ratio is one trainer to one resident. In a small training school or training center, or in the home of a retarded child, this ratio is usually possible. In institutional settings, however, where a majority of a ward's population may be incontinent, a one-to-one ratio is not always possible. If the residents do not have severe behavior problems, i.e., refuse to sit on the toilet or are aggressive, then one trainer can easily instruct three residents simultaneously with only occasional help needed from an assistant during the later stages of training. In fact, when more than one resident is trained at once, there is less chance the trainer will become bored since he will be engaged in training activities during the entire training period. Also, residents can then learn by imitation (see p. 28). Advantages exist for having two trainers assigned to the training program: they can divide their time so that each trains four hours per day and performs other duties at other times; they can observe each other; one can supervise the Maintenance procedure; one can assist with hyperactive residents. Also, the effectiveness of a trainer may wane toward the latter portion of an eight-hour training day if he is not relieved for brief periods.

Which Residents to Train First

Begin the training program with the highest IQ incontinent residents on the ward. With higher IQ residents, slight mistakes that are made in training can usually be corrected without unduly extending the training time. Also, the higher IQ residents do not require the behavior shaping techniques of prompting and fading (see p. 38). If possible, select residents who can dress themselves and who have demonstrated some bladder control in the past. As you become more proficient in your training methods, you can then train residents with lower IQs or behavior problems.

Time Spent Training the Residents Each Day

Training should be conducted for as long as possible each day (hopefully no less than 4 hours), and the trainer should remain in the toilet with the residents during the entire period. The longer the training period is each day, the faster the residents will be toilet trained. During the training the resident is learning that correct toileting is very important but after a training day is over, the ward staff is not able to show this same concern. Consequently, if a long time period passes before the next brief training period, the resident will conclude that the concern over proper toileting is inconsistent and temporary. To be maximally effective, the training program must be uninterrupted. An 8-hour training program should be conducted each day whenever possible.

Learning by Imitation

When several residents are simultaneously receiving training, the process of learning by imitation usually occurs. Imitation simply means that one person will learn by observing another. Psychological studies have shown that individuals will imitate the behavior of an individual who is receiving rewards. For example, if you began rewarding residents for standing beside you, you would quickly find yourself surrounded by residents. Imitation is very helpful during the toilet training program since residents will see each other being rewarded for appropriate toileting behavior and thereby be motivated to toilet themselves correctly.

Preparation of the Toilet

Prior to training, the trainer should bring the following items into the toilet: about 8 pairs of the cotton briefs per resident, a chair for each resident, drinking glasses or cups marked with each resident's name, 3 or 4 different fluids in various containers, a bowl of candies, a kitchen (or pocket) timer,† a small table, a pants alarm for each resident (see p. 31), a urine alert for each toilet (see p. 30), and the Daytime Toilet Training Checklist (See Figure 6, p. 62). Table 1 lists these required materials. Training will be most successful if extraneous influences are minimized; encourage other ward residents and staff members, therefore, to stay out of the toilet. The ideal situation is for the trainer to conduct training with only the residents being trained present. To ensure privacy, have the other residents use another toilet during the training periods. If the ward toilet must be used by other residents, a partition can be placed so that the toilet stools farthest from the doorway can be used for training while the toilet stools closest to the doorway are used by the other ward residents. An alternative to the partitions is to use portable toilets for the other ward residents. These portable toilets may be placed in a shower room or any other suitable room on the ward during the training period.

Table 1   Materials Required for Daytime Training

1.	Cotton briefs with moisture-detecting snaps inserted in the crotch area (p. 32)
2.	Chairs
3.	Urine alerts (p. 29)
4.	Pants alarms (p. 31)
5.	Small table
6.	Variety of fluids (p. 34)
7.	Candies and edibles (p. 33)
8.	Individually marked drinking glasses or cups
9.	Kitchen timer or pocket timer
10.	Cloths
11.	Daytime Toilet Training Checklist (Figure 6, p. 62)

Detection of Eliminations

Appropriate Eliminations

Detecting when the resident has eliminated is not always easy. If it is quiet in the toilet, the sound of the urine hitting the water in the toilet bowl could cue the trainer. However, there may be times when

---

† For ordering information, see p. 135.

not enough urine is expelled to make a detectable sound or when it is not quiet in the toilet since several residents may be receiving training at the same time. Rewarding a resident by mistake when he actually has not urinated only confuses him as does failing to reward him when he has urinated. Since positioning the resident with his legs far enough apart to permit an unobstructed view is uncomfortable, the resident would probably not remain in that position very long. Because of these difficulties, a new method for immedi-

---

Figure 2   The Urine Alert
        The plastic bowl fits into the normal toilet bowl and rests on its top edge. The detachable wires connect the moisture-detecting snaps to the signal box which can rest on the floor or top of the toilet. The signal box sounds a tone when urine or feces touches the snaps.

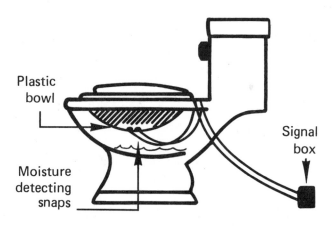

Plastic bowl

Signal box

Moisture detecting snaps

---

ately detecting eliminations is needed. A urine alert † answers this need. It consists of a plastic insert which fits most standard toilet bowls. In the bottom of the urine alert are two moisture-detecting snaps which are connected by wires to a battery-powered signal box

---

† For ordering information, see p. 135.

(see Figure 2). When urine touches the snaps, a tone sounds, which alerts the trainer that the resident has eliminated. To terminate the sound, the urine alert bowl must be completely emptied and the two moisture-sensitive snaps wiped dry with a cloth.

A less immediate but also less expensive means of detecting eliminations is to place a large piece of blue litmus paper † in the ward toilet bowl. Blue litmus paper instantly turns a bright pink when urine touches it. If the trainer can see even a small section of the litmus paper, the pink color will alert him that the resident has urinated. The litmus paper can be flushed down the toilet after each usage. The major advantage of litmus paper is its low cost; its disadvantage is that the trainer must constantly check the toilet bowl. Therefore, it is suggested that litmus paper be used only when one resident is receiving training and when the auditory signaling apparatus cannot be obtained.

Inappropriate Eliminations

Inappropriate eliminations must also be detected as soon as they occur. Immediate detection of accidents allows the trainer to provide an immediate disapproving reaction. A pants alarm † was made expressly for immediately detecting accidents (see Figure 3). The pants alarm consists of a light-weight signal box that is pinned to the resident's underwear. Two wires lead from the signal box, pass between the resident's legs, and attach to moisture-detecting snaps in the crotch region of the underpants. When the resident has an accident, the signal sounds as soon as the urine wets the cloth area between the moisture-detecting snaps.

Blue litmus paper can be used to detect accidents as an alternative to the pants alarm. The paper is taped to the pants in the crotch area.‡ Any brand of adhesive tape should be satisfactory. The first few drops of urine will soak through to the litmus paper, turning it bright pink, which provides the trainer with an immediate visual signal that an accident is occurring. A disadvantage of the paper is that the trainer must attend more closely to the resident's clothing than when using the pants alarm.

Both the urine alert and the pants alarm remove the necessity of the trainer maintaining a constant vigil of one resident, thus allowing the trainer the freedom to work with more residents and to keep the necessary training records. The apparatuses allow immediate detection and reaction to appropriate and inappropriate eliminations. The trainer can then provide the combination of posi-

---

† For ordering information, see p. 135.

‡ Female residents should be required to wear trousers or culottes when using litmus paper.

Figure 3   The Pants Alarm
The front view shows the moisture-detecting snaps
fastened to the briefs. The back view shows the two flexible wires which
lead from the snaps to the signal box. The snaps on the end of the wire
are manually removable from the snaps on the clothing. The signal box
is pinned to the back of the briefs (back view). A tone is sounded by the
signal box when urine or feces moistens the area between the snaps.

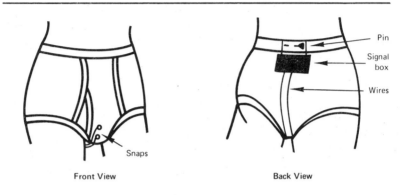

Front View   Back View

tive reactions for appropriate eliminations and disapproving reactions for inappropriate eliminations, both of which are essential in this program.

Use of Underpants or Cotton Briefs

During training, the underpants (pants alarm) must be worn. However, in some institutions, the residents normally do not wear underpants. Such residents must, therefore, be taught to lower and raise this unfamiliar garment when toileting. To simplify the act of toileting, restrictive outer garments should not be worn during training. The residents should not wear trousers (males) or long dresses (females) until they have learned to toilet by themselves while wearing only underpants.

The resident should be wearing cotton briefs containing the moisture-detecting snaps during the training sessions and at no other time. The cotton training briefs should be several sizes larger than what the resident would normally wear, yet small enough at the waist so that they do not slide down the resident's hips. The larger pants make it easier for the resident to pull his pants up and down. If the available briefs are too tight, they may be permanently enlarged by pulling the elastic waistband. If this stretching does not increase the waist size sufficiently, then the waistband may be clipped with scissors. At least 8 pair of briefs per resident should be allotted each day.

Location of the Moisture-Detecting Snaps

To be most effective, the moisture-detecting snaps (p. 31) are placed on the underpants where they are most likely to be dampened by urine. The ideal location varies according to the resident's age and sex. Figure 4 shows the correct clothing snap placement for men, women, and children. Note that the snaps are placed lower in the crotch area for women and children. For men, the snaps should be placed approximately one-half inch below where the penis touches the briefs. The snaps should be approximately one inch apart. A small piece of adhesive tape should be placed over the backs of the snaps as a precaution against the signal sounding because of perspiration from the resident's body.

Figure 4   Correct Placement of the Moisture-Detecting Snaps
Men: the snaps are placed one-half inch below where the penis touches the briefs. Women: the snaps are placed in the lower portion of the crotch area of the briefs. Children: the snaps are placed approximately one inch above the crotch region of the briefs. The snaps should be placed approximately one inch apart in all cases.

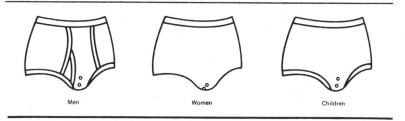

Men   Women   Children

Candies and Treats

Candies and other edible treats are used to reward the resident for successful eliminations and for remaining dry. The amount of edible reward that is given at the dry-pants inspections should be less than the amount given for successful voiding (see p. 44). The edible reward for dry pants should be small and approximately bite-sized, for example, an M&M candy. The edible reward for voiding, in contrast, should be quite large, for example, one-third of a candy bar or 10 M&M candies. A large reward for voiding increases the resident's motivation to toilet himself. By providing the resident with a piece of candy together with verbal praise you are indicating to him that he has pleased you. The resident will learn that correct toileting pleases you and that you, in turn, will please him. A few days after training, it will no longer be necessary for you to provide candy, so have no concern about the resident becoming overly dependent on candy as a reward. The exact details of how and when to give candy are described later in the sections dealing with Training (p. 60; Figure 6, p. 62) and Maintenance (p. 71).

Increased Consumption of Fluids

Urinations and defecations usually occur about six to ten times in the course of a day for incontinent retardates. As a result, there are only these six to ten opportunities each day to teach the resident correct usage of the toilet. This low frequency accounts, in part, for the long period of time usually required for the acquisition of proper toilet habits. This problem can be avoided, however, by encouraging the resident to drink as much fluid as he can comfortably consume. By giving the resident unlimited access to fluids, he will have more urinations which will provide more opportunities during training to teach correct toileting. Because females generally urinate more often than males, they will probably have both more appropriate and inappropriate eliminations than do males.

During training, several different fluids should be available to the resident, for example, coffee, tea, soft drinks such as cola and ginger ale, water, milk, fruit juices, and punches. Coffee and tea are especially appropriate since they are diuretics. However, the adult resident should not receive more than 6 to 8 cups since large amounts of these caffeine drinks can upset the stomach. Some residents will easily drink as many as 10 cups of fluid in an hour. This increased consumption of non-caffeinated fluids is not harmful, since most residents will drink only as much as they feel comfortable consuming. If the resident does not spontaneously stop drinking, allow him about 4 cups per half-hour. Should the resident refuse to drink even moderate amounts, prompt him by verbally encouraging him to take a small sip, and by placing the cup against his lips so that the fluid touches the lips. The taste of the fluid will often prime the resident into taking a sip.

Reducing the Resident's Intake of Fluids at Day's End

Two hours before the end of the training day, limit the residents' intake of fluids by allowing *no more* than 2 cups of fluid per half-hour. During the last hour of training, the residents should be allowed only 2 or 3 swallows of fluid per half-hour. Reducing the amount of fluid the residents receive will reduce the number of accidents they will have after the day's training has been completed.

34

CHAPTER 4

TRAINING

Overview of the Training

Training occurs in two phases. The first phase trains the resident to control his bladder and bowel muscles so that he eliminates only when he is seated on the toilet. This phase is commonly called habit or bladder training. There are two indicators that bladder control has been achieved: (1) the absence of accidents during the training period since the resident is exerting bladder control by not relaxing his bladder sphincter until he sits on the toilet and (2) elimination shortly after the resident sits on the toilet. The immediate elimination indicates that the resident "understands" the purpose of the toilet. If the resident sits for several minutes before eliminating, he probably does not yet understand what he is to do on the toilet seat. Sitting on the toilet has not yet become associated with the act of eliminating. When a resident has bladder control, it does not imply that he toilets without prompting, that he has the dressing skills, or that he is normally motivated to stay dry. It means only that he can control his bladder, but not that he does so in a normal social situation. The successful completion of the bladder training phase, therefore, does not ensure that the resident will begin independently toileting himself. The second phase of toilet training is independent toileting, wherein the resident *self-initiates* his own toileting performance without any reminders.

Graduated Guidance

When teaching a high IQ retardate a new skill, the simplest and usual method is to give verbal instructions on how the skill should be performed. For example, to teach a resident how to flush a toilet, the trainer would tell the resident to put his hand on the flush-handle and to press down hard for a short period. After the resident has followed these instructions, the trainer rewards him thereby providing motivation. The next time, the trainer need only remind the resident to perform the act, without the need to repeat the details of how to do it, and the resident will have the understanding and motivation to do so.

Manual Guidance

A very low IQ retardate usually does not have completely developed language and consequently cannot understand simple instructions well enough to carry them out. In this case, manual guidance, whereby the trainer grasps the resident's hand and moves it through the proper motions, is used as a substitute for verbal instructions. The trainer then rewards the resident at the completion of the guided act, just as he would when using verbal instructions.

The ultimate objective of instruction is that the resident will be able and motivated to carry out the instructed task by himself. Therefore, the trainer must use some method of having the resident carry out the complete act without any manual guidance. The procedure for eliminating the need for manual guidance is *fading* and consists of a progressive reduction in the amount of manual guidance until the point is reached where none is used. Fading is usually carried out by using less guidance on each successive trial. On the first trial, the resident's hand is grasped firmly, but on the next trial less firmly, on the next very gently, and so on until not even a touch is needed. After many trials, the manual guidance will have faded out.

Several problems are frequently encountered in fading out the manual guidance. First, the resident may be very passive and his hands will be limp such that the trainer is supplying all of the effort while the resident is not attempting to contribute to the movement. When the trainer decreases the guidance on the next trial, he finds that no motion results. On the next trial he must, therefore, return to the increased level of guidance if the act is to be completed. The resident in this instance has become dependent on the trainer since he seems to believe that he should wait for the trainer to do all of the work. The result is that a very large number of trials will be needed to fade out the manual guidance.

A second problem in using manual guidance is encountered with the resident who resists the trainer's effort to move his hands. The resistance may be a part of a general negative reaction to staff efforts. It may be a result of the resident's mistaken belief that the trainer is attempting to harm or to overcome him. Or, the resident may resist because of confusion as to what the trainer desires. Whatever the cause of the initial resistance to manual guidance, the resident will often become emotional, disturbed, and even violent if the trainer continues to manually guide him while he is resisting. This emotional state prevents the trainer from continuing the instruction.

A third problem in fading out manual guidance is that a number of trials are needed, often a large number. This problem exists even when the resident is neither overly passive nor resistive.

36

As noted above, the trainer exerts a specific amount of force on a particular trial, then on the next trial a lesser amount, and still less on the next trial. Since fading occurs from one trial to the next, a number of trials must be given for successful fading.

Graduated Guidance

An alternative to manual guidance is the graduated guidance technique which reduces the above three problems. Graduated guidance is used for the same reason that manual guidance was used: to teach a skill to a retardate who cannot understand instructions by manually guiding him through the proper motions. The difference between the two techniques is that with graduated guidance the amount of hand pressure is adjusted at each moment, depending on the resident's performance at that moment. The graduated guidance procedure is used in the following manner:

1. Exert no more force at any given moment than is needed to move the resident's hand in the desired direction.

2. At the start of each trial, use the minimal force (even a touch) and build up until the hand starts moving.

3. Once the hand starts to move, decrease the guidance instantly and gradually as long as the guided hand continues to move.

4. If movement stops during a trial, increase the guiding force instantly and gradually to the point where movement again results.

5. If the guided hand pushes against you in the direction away from the proper motion, apply just enough force to counteract that force, thereby keeping the resisting hand in a non-moving position.

6. As soon as the resisting hand decreases the degree of opposing force, instantly decrease the amount of force so that the resident's resistance is again just being counterbalanced.

7. When the guided hand stops actively resisting, immediately but gradually start again to use just enough force to move the guided hand.

8. Once a trial starts, continue to guide the hand until the response is completed; do not give up or interrupt before the final step.

9. At the end of the trial, give a reward.

10. The reward should be given together with the desired physical effect produced by the completion of the response.

11. When the reward is about to be given at the completion of the response, eliminate the guidance by withdrawing even touch contact and then give the reward.

12. Verbal praise should also be given during the guidance but only at those moments when the resident is actively participating in the movement and never while he is resisting or completely passive.

Shadowing. When guidance has been faded out to a mere touch, shadowing, the next lower level of guidance is used. The trainer's hand follows the resident's hand at a distance of a fraction of an inch but not touching.

Spatial fading. An equally acceptable alternative to shadowing as a means of fading out touch contact is spatial fading. It is conducted by first decreasing the guiding force on the resident's hand to a mere touch, then by moving the touch contact to the wrist, the forearm, the elbow, the upper arm and then finally to the shoulder and back within each trial.

Prompt-Fading of Toilet Approach

The prompting technique is crucial for teaching the resident to toilet himself, and requires great skill and thought from the trainer. A prompt is a cue to the resident that you want him to do something and it can be either verbal or gestural. A verbal prompt consists simply of instructions. Gestural prompts consist of pointing in a particular direction, touching the resident, looking toward a particular spot, etc. The resident must be prompted regularly during the initial part of training but not at all during the final part. Consequently, great care is needed to use the minimal amount of prompting at every stage. For higher IQ retardates, prompting is generally necessary only on the first few training trials, after which the individual normally does what is expected without further prompts. For retardates with lower IQs or behavioral disorders, however, prompts are used for an extended period, especially when teaching a complex sequence of behaviors. The advantage of a prompt is that it initiates a behavior that can then be rewarded. The disadvantage is that the individual becomes dependent on the prompts and on the prompter. Should the trainer ever fail to remind (prompt) the resident to toilet, the resident will have an accident. Thus, while prompts are beneficial in teaching, they should be faded out as quickly as possible so that the resident will initiate toileting even when the trainer is absent.

Prompts range from very faint, almost indiscernible prompts to very active and conspicuous prompts. The more conspicuous a prompt, the less reason the prompted individual has to rely on his own memory and motivation. The general goal, then, is to fade out this dependence by fading out the prompts. Prompts can

38

be reduced by using fading whereby the trainer gives a less active prompt each time than he gave previously. For example, the first time the resident is prompted to the toilet, the trainer may touch him on the shoulder and point to the toilet. The next time the resident is prompted, the trainer would just point to the toilet—he has faded out touching the resident on the shoulder. The trainer has gone from actual physical contact with the resident to just pointing to the direction of the toilet. By fading, the trainer approaches the time when no prompt will be given and the resident will have to decide to self-initiate his toileting.

Fading verbal prompts is generally done in two ways: either by reducing the number of words in an instruction or by progressively softening the tone in which the instruction is given. A full toileting prompt would consist of telling the resident to go to the toilet and providing whatever graduated guidance is necessary to guide him there (see p. 37). Prompts should be faded by first eliminating all verbal prompts (instructions), and then eliminating all gestural prompts. The reason for this is that verbal prompts are more difficult to fade out in a gradual way. The upper

---

Table 2   Toilet-Approach Prompts*

General Guidelines

1. Determine the minimal prompt the resident responds to. This may be a touch, pointing toward the toilet, or an instruction.

2. Use a less active prompt the next time the resident is prompted to the toilet.

3. Wait a few seconds after the prompt before giving graduated guidance.

4. The sequence of toileting prompts are listed below from most active to least active. The resident will usually begin independently toileting himself before the least active prompt is given.

Sequence of Steps

Prompt	Example
1. Verbal instruction	"John, go to the toilet."
+	
Gesture	Point to the toilet.
+	
Touch	Lightly tug at resident's shirt (guide him from his chair to the toilet if necessary).
2. Verbal instruction	"John, go to the toilet."
+	
Gesture	Point to the toilet.
No touch	

---

3. Reduced verbal instruction + Gesture No touch	"John, toilet." Point to the toilet.
4.ª Reduced verbal instruction + Gesture No touch	"Toilet." Point to the toilet.
5. No verbal instruction Gesture No touch	Point to the toilet with your arm fully extended and motion toward the toilet with your head.
6. No verbal instruction Reduced gesture No touch	Point to the toilet with your arm partially extended and full head motion.
7. No verbal instruction Reduced gesture (no arm motion) No touch	Point to the toilet with full head motion.
8. No verbal instruction Reduced gesture No touch	Motion toward the toilet with your head.
9. No verbal instruction Reduced gesture (no head motion) No touch	Move your eyes toward the toilet.

portion of Table 2 presents some general guidelines to be used in prompting a resident to the toilet; the lower portion presents the order in which prompts should be faded. The prompts are arranged with the most active at the top decreasing to the least active at the bottom.

When the trainer has reached the phase where slight arm, head, and eye movements are effective, the fading process will usually occur naturally thereafter without the need for the trainer to consciously decrease the size of the gesture. This natural fading occurs because the trainer's head and arms are normally moving about. Consequently, the gestural prompt blends naturally into this movement background and the resident is less able to depend on the movements as a reminder of the trainer's desires. He then begins relying on his own memory and desires.

Starting Level of Prompting

Earlier it was suggested that one of the advantages of training for a long period each day is that the residents have repeated opportunities to learn appropriate toileting behavior. When the training day ends, however, sixteen hours or more will elapse before the resident again receives training. Since retardates have difficulty remembering over time, it is important to begin each resident's instruction with the last prompt that he successfully responded to on the previous day. It may even be necessary to move back one step, giving a more obvious prompt. For example, if at the end of the first training day, the resident was going to the toilet when the trainer told him to and pointed to the toilet (see Table 2, Step 2), the trainer would begin the second day's training with Step 2. If the resident failed to respond to a Step 2 prompt, the trainer would back up to Step 1 where the trainer also *touches* the resident. *Start each training day using prompts that the resident successfully responded to on the previous day.*

Toilet-Related Dressing Skills

Independent toileting requires that the residents be able to raise and lower their pants. Yet, many residents have not yet learned to dress themselves and are unable to raise and lower their pants. Often, these residents are dressed by one of the ward staff or by a higher functioning resident from another ward. Residents who already know how to dress themselves usually proceed through training faster and should be considered first as candidates for toilet training. The trainers may, therefore, wish to train dressing prior to initiating the toilet training program. Alternatively, residents can be trained to raise and lower their pants during the toilet training procedure.

Prompting, fading of prompting, and graduated guidance are the principal techniques used to teach the skills of raising and lowering the pants. The techniques are used in a similar manner as that described for teaching the resident to approach the toilet. Adult males and children should have their shirts rolled or pinned up approximately two inches above the waistband of their pants so that the shirt does not cover the waistband of the pants, causing difficulty for the resident in locating the waistband. The sequence of training steps is nearly the same for both sexes; however, female residents (1) must first reach up under their dresses before grasping their underpants and (2) have only to lower one set of pants. Otherwise, lowering and raising of pants is taught in the sequence of steps listed in the lower portion of Table 3. The upper portion of Table 3 presents general guidelines to be used in training the resident to raise and lower his pants. The steps in raising and lowering the pants are presented separately. The prompting steps are arranged

Table 3   Prompts for Raising and Lowering Pants*

General Guidelines

1. Determine the minimal prompt the resident responds to. This may be a touch, pointing to his pants, or a verbal instruction.

2. Use a less active prompt the next time the resident is prompted to pull his pants up or down.

3. Wait a few seconds after the prompt before giving graduated guidance.

4. The sequence of dressing prompts are listed below from most active to least active. The resident will usually begin independently raising or lowering his pants before the least active prompt is given.

Sequence of Steps for Pulling Pants Down

Note: The resident should pull his pants down below his knees.

Prompt	Example
1. Verbal instruction	"John, pants down."
+	
Gesture	Point to resident's pants.
+	
Touch	Grasp resident's hands around the waistband of his pants and use graduated guidance to guide him in pulling them down.
2. Reduced verbal instruction	"Pants down."
+	
Gesture	Point to resident's pants.
+	
Touch	Grasp resident's hands around the waistband of his pants if necessary and use graduated guidance to guide him in pulling them down.
3. Reduced verbal instruction	"Down."
+	
Gesture	Point to resident's pants.
+	
Reduced touch	Guide resident's hands to the waistband of his pants if necessary.
4. No verbal instruction	
Reduced gesture	Look at resident's pants.
+	
Touch, if necessary	Guide resident's hands to waistband if necessary.

5. No verbal instruction

   Reduced gesture   Look at resident's pants.

   No touch

Sequence of Steps for Pulling Pants Up

Note: Since the resident's pants are below his knees, it will be easier for him to pull
   them up if he bends forward slightly.

Prompt	Example
1. Verbal instruction +	"John, pants up."
Gesture +	Point to resident's pants.
Touch	Place your hands over resident's hands and use graduated guidance to guide his hands to the waistband of his pants and to pull them up.
2. Reduced verbal instruction +	"Pants up."
Gesture +	Point to resident's pants.
Touch	Grasp resident's hands around the waistband of his pants and use graduated guidance to guide him in pulling them up.
3. Reduced verbal instruction +	"Up."
Gesture +	Point to resident's pants.
Reduced touch	Guide resident's hands to waistband if necessary.
4. No verbal instruction	
Reduced gesture +	Look at resident's pants.
Touch, if necessary	Guide resident's hands to waistband if necessary.
5. No verbal instruction	
Gesture	Look at resident's pants.
No touch	

---

with the most active prompts at the top decreasing to the least active prompts at the bottom. This arrangement of prompts represents the order in which the prompts should be faded.

As was the case in teaching the resident to approach the toilet (p. 38), the fading process will usually occur naturally once the trainer has reached the phase where slight gestures are effective in prompting the resident to raise or lower his pants since the gestural prompt blends in with the trainer's natural movements. Again, the resident is less able to depend on prompts and, therefore, must begin relying on his own memory and initiative.

Flushing the Toilet

During the toilet training, the residents are taught to flush the toilet as the final step in toileting. The techniques of prompting, fading of prompting, and graduated guidance are all used. The resident is taught to flush the toilet immediately after he has raised his pants. (Since the urine is in the urine alert bowl, the flushing action will not cause the urine to flush down the toilet bowl. Consequently, the trainer leaves the urine alert in place until the resident has been directed back to his chair. The trainer then empties the contents of the urine alert into the toilet bowl and flushes the toilet.) Teaching the resident to flush the toilet after he voids (even though the urine alert is in place) ensures that he will continue to flush the toilet when his training is completed and the urine alert is no longer preventing the urine from being flushed normally. Usually, no edible reward is needed to motivate the resident to flush the toilet, since the sound produced by the flushing action is often rewarding in itself. Praise, however, should be given immediately for flushing. It is especially important that this skill be developed in low IQ retardates since an unflushed toilet may encourage feces smearing or coprophagy by some residents.

The Actual Bladder Training Sequence

Approximately one hour prior to training, the ward staff should begin giving fluids to the residents. The residents should then benefit from the initial part of training since they will be ready to urinate as soon as training begins. Therefore, the training period should start with a successful elimination.

Begin training by attaching the small pants alarms to the residents' briefs and then seat the residents on the chairs which have been brought to the bathroom. The chairs should be approximately three feet from the toilet. The urine alert bowls should be placed in the toilet bowl at this time. Begin training on the half-hour (e.g., 9:00 or 9:30) since it is easier to keep track of time. Table 4 shows the sequence of steps to be followed in bladder training.

Begin training by offering the resident a drink. Allow him to drink several cups of fluid and then pause for one minute.

Use graduated guidance to teach the resident to approach the toilet bowl. Call the resident by name and tell him to "Go to the toilet" and point at the toilet bowl. If he makes no attempt to move toward the toilet bowl, gently tug at his shirt to prompt him off the chair and then orient him in the desired direction. Follow

Table 4   Sequence of Steps in the Bladder Training Procedure (Start exactly on the half-hour)

1. Give as much fluid to the resident as he will drink while seated in his chair.
   a. Wait about 1 minute.
2. Direct resident to sit on toilet seat using the minimal possible prompt.
3. Direct resident to pull his pants down using the minimal possible prompt.
4. a. When resident voids, give edible and praise while seated, then direct him to stand.
   b. If resident does not void within 20 minutes after drinking the fluids, direct him to stand.
5. Direct resident to pull up his pants using the minimal possible prompt.
   a. If resident voided, direct him to flush the toilet using the minimal possible prompt.
6. Direct resident to his chair using the minimal possible prompt.
7. After resident has been sitting for 5 minutes, inspect him for dry pants.
   a. If pants are dry, give edible and praise.
   b. If pants are wet, only show him the edible and admonish him.
8. Check resident for dry pants every 5 minutes.
9. At the end of 30 minutes, begin the sequence of steps again.

Note: 1. If self-initiation occurs at any time, turn to page 53 and start the self-initiation procedure.
2. Continuously praise resident for being dry while he is seated in his chair.

the resident and provide graduated guidance should he stop moving. Once the resident reaches the toilet bowl, tell him, "Pants down." Should he fail to respond, place your hands over his and tuck his hands around the waist of the pants so that he has a firm grip on the pants. Gently guide his hands with your hands and as he begins the desired movement, reduce the guidance. The next time the resident is prompted to the toilet he should be given even less help. When the resident's pants are lowered, prompt him to sit on the toilet. He should remain on the toilet for 20 minutes or until he voids. You should then prompt another resident to a toilet and so forth until all the residents are on the toilets. As soon as the resi-

45

dent eliminates, he should be given a large piece of candy and praised, e.g., "You are such a big boy!" and hugged.

The resident should then be encouraged to stand up. Tell him to stand up; if he does not, gently tug at his shirt and use graduated guidance to guide him manually. Once he is standing, prompt him to pull his pants up. If he fails to respond, use graduated guidance to manually guide his hands in pulling up his pants just as you did for pulling the pants down. If the resident voided, he is prompted and guided in flushing the toilet. With the completion of dressing and flushing the toilet, the resident may return to his chair. The trainer should continuously interact with the resident during the time he·is off the toilet seat. Every 5 minutes, the resident should be asked if his pants are dry, made to feel the crotch of his pants (the resident will learn to feel the difference between wet and dry pants), and given a small piece of candy and praise, if his pants are dry (see Table 5). The bladder training sequence is repeated every 30 minutes. Less physical assistance should be needed at each step.

Table 5   Dry-Pants Inspection Procedure During Bladder Training*
(Every 5 minutes unless interrupted by an accident)

1. Ask resident if he is dry. Example: "John, are you dry?"
2. Place resident's hands on the crotch region of his pants so that he is showing that he is dry.
3. Have resident look at his pants.
4. If the pants are dry, give the resident his edible reward and praise him. Example: "John, you're a good boy; you have dry pants."
5. If the pants are wet, or an accident occurred since the last check period, show the resident the reward and admonish him. Example: "John, you can't have any candy because you wet your pants."

The prompting-fading procedure should be used on successive trials to eliminate the need for the various verbal and gestural prompts. For example, saying "Go to the toilet" is reduced to "Toilet," then to merely pointing at the toilet, and then reduced to just a glance. At some point during this reduction of prompts on each successive trial, the resident will independently rise and toilet himself. Following this first self-initiation, *no further toilet-approach prompts should be given*. Similarly, for the act of pulling the pants down, pulling them back up, and sitting on the toilet seat, do not give any further prompts once the resident has initiated any one of these acts without a prompt.

The training procedure is sequential: fluids every 30 minutes, toileting, reward following appropriate elimination, 5-minute dry-pants inspections with a reward for dry pants. The training sequence is interrupted only when an accident occurs (see p. 48). Figure 5 shows a flow, chart of the bladder training sequence.

Figure 5   Flow Chart of the Bladder Training Sequence

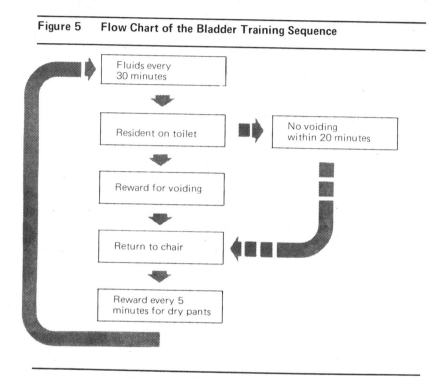

The Use of Lunch as a Reward

When the training program is scheduled to last through lunch, the residents should not be given their lunch to eat all at once. In order to maintain the residents' motivation, their lunches should be used as rewards during the dry-pants inspections. By giving the resident a spoonful of his lunch when his pants are dry at each inspection, the lunch can be used as a reward for several hours during the afternoon. If you do not wish to use bites of the lunch as rewards, divide the lunch into about 6 portions and allow the resident to eat one portion at each of the next 6 dry-pants inspections. This procedure is not as preferable as using spoon-sized portions.

Accidents During Bladder Training

Accidents during training in the toilet area are to be expected but discouraged. As soon as the pants alarm signals that a resident has wet, the trainer should immediately go to the resident, and say, "No, you wet your pants" and show a displeased expression. The trainer should obtain the resident's attention to this displeased expression, if necessary, by grasping the resident's shoulders and orienting him to look at the trainer. The wires connected to the clothing snaps should be disconnected and the resident required to clean up or wipe up any traces of urine on the floor or chair. No other attention should be paid to the accident except to verbally instruct the resident in cleaning up and to tell him that you are displeased. Table 6 lists the sequence of steps in the Brief Cleanliness Training Procedure During Bladder Training.

Immediately following Brief Cleanliness Training, the resident should be required to practice appropriate toileting behaviors. This required practice is designated as Positive Practice Training and is designed to ensure that the resident learns the acceptable alternative to wetting his clothing (see Table 7). The Positive Prac-

---

Table 6   Brief Cleanliness Training Procedure During Bladder Training*
(Accident signaled by the pants alarm)

---

1. Immediately grasp the resident by the shoulders so that he is looking at you.

2. Tell the resident, "No, you wet your pants" and show displeasure on your face.

3. Disconnect the wires from the clothing snaps.

4. Require resident to clean up any traces of urine on the floor or chair.

---

tice Training consists of the following steps: the resident is required by instructions and graduated guidance to walk to the toilet stool from his chair, lower his pants, sit on the toilet stool for a few seconds, arise, raise his pants, and return to his chair. The Positive Practice Training is repeated for several trials without interruption until the next half-hour's regularly scheduled toileting. The instructions and physical guidance should be faded on each succeeding trial. If the resident voids in the toilet during a Positive Practice trial, *do not* reward him; his voiding should be ignored. However, should a self-initiated approach be made to the toilet, definitely reward the resident as usual at the moment of voiding. At the end of each Positive Practice trial, a dry-pants inspection is made; the resident is to be guided in feeling his wet pants, and shown the snack but denied it with a short explanation that he has soiled his pants and, therefore, is not eligible for candy at that time. Fluids are not given prior to the next scheduled toileting, since fluids also serve as a reward. The resident's pants are not changed immediately after an accident because he must learn to associate wet pants with the

---

Table 7   Positive Practice for Daytime Accidents
During Toilet Training*
(Given immediately following Brief Cleanliness Training)

---

1. Require resident to walk rapidly to the toilet stool from his chair.

2. Require resident to lower his pants, sit on toilet stool for a few seconds, arise, raise his pants, and return to his chair.

Repeat the above steps for several trials without interruption until the next half-hour's regularly scheduled toileting. Use verbal instructions and graduated guidance, if necessary, fading them on each succeeding trial.

---

trainer's disapproval and with the absence of praise and rewards, which would otherwise have been given continually for dry pants. He should change his clothes at the completion of the next scheduled toilet-approach trial (when he rises from the toilet at the end of 20 minutes or after having voided). The pants alarm is also reconnected at this time.

What Happens to the Resident
at the End of the Training Day

No special treatment should be given the resident after the day's training has been completed since he has not yet been completely toilet trained. The resident will almost certainly have several accidents during the remainder of the day since he has consumed a large quantity of fluids during his training. The toilet trainer will have anticipated this problem and partially solved it by reducing the amount of fluids offered during the last few hours before the end of the day's training (see Reducing Fluids, p. 34) but the resident may still have some accidents that evening. Since the resident has not completed his training, he cannot be held entirely responsible so only a brief type of Cleanliness Training should be used at this time. When the resident is found wet, the ward staff should require that he change his own clothing, clean up any traces of the accident, and clean himself up with a dry towel. Graduated guidance should be given if the resident refuses or is unable to change his own clothing, clean himself up, or wipe up the spot he has made. The staff should instruct the resident in neutral tones. The resident may be somewhat resistive, since he has had a long history of the staff taking care of his needs such as changing his clothing when he has soiled. This brief form of Cleanliness Training is the only requirement of the ward staff during the toilet training program; this brief corrective activity introduces the resident to accepting the responsibility for cleaning up his accidents.

Toilet Training the Resident Who Already Has Some Toileting Skills

Follow the same sequence of steps for the resident who already has some control over his toileting as for the resident who has shown none of the required skills for self-toileting. Regardless of prior training, all residents should receive the same sequence of steps in the toilet training program since the program is designed such that the trainer can determine within one or two trials that a given skill is present, and, if so, go on to the next step. If the skill is not present, the trainer will not mistakenly make impossible demands; if it is present, the trainer will have spent only one or two trials at the most in determining its presence. For example, if the resident already has bladder control, and knows the purpose of the toilet, the trainer will see that he is eliminating shortly after sitting on the toilet stool and does so on each of the toilet-approach trials. The trainer will then emphasize such skills as dressing and unprompted toilet-approach with little time lost.

Training Bowel Control

The primary emphasis of the toilet training procedure is on urination. Since bowel movements are almost always preceded by urination, the training for proper urination will also produce proper habits for defecation. This parallel training is maximized by training the resident to urinate in the seated position, which is, of course, the normal position for proper bowel movements. Otherwise, if the male residents were taught to urinate while standing, they would have to receive a separate training program to teach bowel control. After a male has successfully self-initiated for several months, he can easily be taught the traditional male stance when urinating. To further ensure that bowel training will result, react to the bowel movements which occur during training in the exact same manner as you react to urinations. For example, if the resident has a bowel movement in the toilet, reward him with candy and praise. If the resident has a bowel movement in his pants, require him to clean himself up with a damp washcloth, to wash out the soil from his pants, to place his soiled pants in the dirty clothes hamper, and to dress himself in clean pants. There is the possibility, however, that training will be accomplished so rapidly that the resident will not have had a bowel movement during the training period. This is not a problem since a resident who is self-initiating each time he has to urinate will eventually have a bowel movement while sitting on the toilet. The increased consumption of fluids during training sometimes results in bowel movements that are loose in consistency. This should not be a source of alarm because the residents' stools will soon return to normal consistency following training.

CHAPTER 5

SELF-INITIATION TRAINING

The most important act in independent toileting is to interrupt one's current activity and start toward the toilet without being prompted. Unfortunately, this is also the weakest part of the toileting sequence since the satisfaction of voiding properly and being rewarded for it is very remote in time. In addition, this act of starting toward the toilet involves an interruption of other activities or thoughts; for the other steps in toileting, namely dressing, undressing, and sitting on the toilet, interruption of those competing activities has already occurred. Consequently, once the resident makes his first genuine attempt to toilet without being prompted, a turning point has been reached in the training and several changes in the guidelines are made at this time. For once the resident has made the single self-initiation, we now have assurance that he understands that he should toilet himself and will be rewarded for doing so. He need not be guided and prompted in the slow careful manner necessary before he had this understanding. From this moment on, the resident assumes greater responsibility and independence. Table 8 outlines the several changes that are made in the training procedure after the first self-initiation. The specific step-by-step changes are shown in Figure 6, Part 4, p. 63.

Now that the resident understands the desirability of toileting himself, the frequency of rewarding the resident for correct toileting can be reduced. Consequently, the rewards for urinating in the toilet bowl are progressively eliminated. After several self-initiations, the trainer allows correct urinations to occur without giving a reward (see the Daytime Toilet Training Checklist, Figure 6, Part 4, p. 63).

The general rules for fading the prompts and guidance are also changed at this point. Since the resident has indicated by his first self-initiation that he understands the appropriate sequence of acts, it is not as necessary to painstakingly require him to progress through the entire sequence every half-hour and with as much guidance and prompting as was needed prior to the self-initiation. The resident is now perfectly free to toilet very infrequently. *Prompting and guidance are never given at a level greater than that needed on previous toiletings,* as was done prior to the first self-initiation. If the previous level of guidance is not sufficient to result in correct toilet-

---

**Table 8   Self-Initiation Training Summary
(After a resident has initiated his own toileting without
a prompt)**

---

1. Give fluids immediately following an elimination.

2. No further toilet-approach prompts are given.

3. Continue to provide guidance and prompts for dressing and undressing and for flushing the toilet, if necessary, but never at a level greater than that needed on previous toiletings (p. 41).

4. Move resident's chair farther from the toilet after each successful self-initiation.

5. Gradually lengthen the time between dry-pants inspections (Table 9, p. 56).

6. Intermittently reward correct toileting (see Daytime Toilet Training Checklist, p. 62).

7. When resident is self-initiating from the area where he spends most of his time, remove urine alert from the toilet bowl, pants alarm from resident's briefs, and the chair.

8. Require resident to show you that he can find the toilet from various areas on the ward.

9. Include resident on the Maintenance Program after 9 self-initiations (Daytime Toilet Training Checklist, p. 62).

---

ing, the resident is returned to his chair. For example, the resident may walk from his chair to the toilet stool, but not lower his pants. The trainer should not prompt or guide the resident to lower his pants if prompts or guidance had not been needed previously for him to do so. If, however, the resident had been requiring a gesture or touch on the wrist before lowering his pants, the trainer should continue to provide this gesture or touch contact if needed before returning the resident to his chair. Under no circumstances should he provide a higher level prompt or guidance such as telling the resident to lower his pants or guiding the resident's hand. This rule applies in the same manner to all the steps in toileting—lowering the pants, sitting on the toilet, arising, raising the pants, and returning to the chair.

The distance that the resident must walk to reach the toilet bowl should be increased now that he understands that he should walk to the toilet by himself. Starting with the first self-initiation, the resident's chair is moved about two feet away from the toilet bowl after each self-initiation. This increased distance will soon bring the chair into the corridor area, after which the chair should be moved toward the general area where the resident spends most of his time. Then the chair is eliminated from the training. By this time the resident no longer depends on prompts for toileting himself at any step. Instead, the trainer then takes the resident to each area of the ward and asks him to find the toilet so that the trainer is assured that he knows how to find the toilet from any place on the ward. During these direction-finding trials, the resident does not normally toilet, nor is he given rewards; consequently, the trainer's instructions do not reestablish the dependency on prompts for future toiletings.

Just as the reward for toileting in the toilet bowl is faded out after the first self-initiation, so is the reward given during the dry-pants inspections on the chair. By the time of the first self-initiation, the resident has been given many of these rewards for being dry and has probably had the opposite experience of no rewards for being wet if he has had an accident. His self-initiation means that he has associated dryness with trainer approval. Start, therefore, reducing the rewards for dryness by increasing the time intervals between dry-pants inspections in the manner outlined in Table 9. The dry-pants inspections are made less and less frequently up to a duration of 2 hours.

Fluids should also be given such that they do not become an unintended prompt for starting toward the toilet. Prior to the first self-initiation, fluids were given every half-hour about one minute prior to prompting the resident. If fluids continue being given every half-hour, the resident may interpret the offer of the drinks as a prompt to go to the toilet. Therefore, give fluids immediately after the resident self-initiates. By giving the drinks then, they will be associated with a low desire to urinate and will not act as a prompt.

The final change in the guidelines is the addition of the Full Cleanliness Training when the resident has an accident.

Full Cleanliness Training for Accidents

Prior to the first self-initiation, only Brief Cleanliness Training was given (see p. 48) because the resident had not learned the correct behavior of toileting himself and consequently should not receive an overly negative reaction. Now that the correct behavior has been learned, the resident should be given Full Cleanliness Training. This procedure has two functions: (1) it teaches responsibility since the resident is required to correct the detrimental effects of his own inappropriate behavior, and (2) it serves as a negative reaction to the accident thereby motivating the resident to toilet himself and remain

---

Table 9   Increased Time Intervals Between Dry-Pants Inspections During Self-Initiation Training

---

Following Self-Initiation Number:	Time Interval
1	Every 5 minutes
2	Every 10 minutes
3	Every 20 minutes
4	Every 30 minutes
5	Every 45 minutes
6	Every 60 minutes
7	Every 90 minutes
8	Every 120 minutes
9	Every 120 minutes

---

dry in order to avoid the nuisance of having to clean up his accidents. Full Cleanliness Training should be given immediately following an accident for 30 minutes. This long period is desirable to ensure that the resident will recall the need for cleaning up if he fails to go to the toilet. The Full Cleaniness Training corrects and overcorrects the effects of the accident. The trainer should instruct the resident in firm but neutral tones. Full Cleanliness Training is conducted in the sequence of steps shown in Table 10. When more than one resident is being trained at one time, the trainer cannot take the time to conduct the Full Cleanliness Training on one of the residents. He should have his assistant trainer conduct it, if he has an assistant. Or, he should have the Maintenance Supervisor conduct it since this Full Cleanliness Training after the first self-initiation is the same procedure the Maintenance Supervisor is conducting during Maintenance (p. 74).

Table 10   Full Cleanliness Training Procedure*

Have the resident clean up his accident by requiring him to:

1. Obtain a mop and mop bucket from their usual location, fill the bucket with water and disinfectant, and take the mop and bucket to the area where he wet or was discovered to be wet.

2. Mop up the accident, wringing out the mop himself.

3. Empty the bucket in the appropriate place, rinse it out, and return it to its usual location.

4. Clean the mop and return it to its usual location.

5. Go to the clothing room and obtain his own dry pants.

6. Carry his dry pants to the shower room or bathroom where he should clean his genital region with a cloth and change into his dry pants.

7. Carry his wet pants to a sink where he should completely immerse them in water, wring them out, and hang them up to dry. (optional)

Use instructions and graduated guidance during the above steps if necessary.

A period of Positive Practice should follow the Full Cleanliness Training in order to ensure that the resident has not had an accident because he has forgotten his previous training (see Table 11). The Positive Practice Training is given immediately following completion of Cleanliness Training. In the Positive Practice procedure, the resident, while dressed in clean clothing, goes to the toilet from where he was discovered wet, lowers his pants, sits on the stool a few seconds, arises, raises his pants, and returns to his chair. Repeat the Positive Practice procedure 6 times. *Do not reward or praise during this required practice.* If necessary, use graduated guidance (p. 37) to gently guide the resident in practicing the act of going to the toilet area.

Resistance to Cleaning Up Accidents

A central feature in teaching independent toileting is the realization by the resident that he has the personal responsibility for cleaning up his accidents. Understandably, if the resident has not been given this expectation, he may be reluctant to accept this responsibility and may resist the staff's reasonable requirement that he must clean up. The general procedure used to overcome this initial reluctance is the graduated guidance procedure (see p. 37) which guides the resident through the proper movements. The trainer is gentle at

---

Table 11   Positive Practice for Daytime Accidents During Self-Initiation Training*
During Self-Initiation Training*
(Given immediately following Full Cleanliness Training)

---

1. Require resident, while dressed in clean clothing, to walk to the toilet stool from where he was discovered wet.

2. Require resident to lower his pants, sit on toilet stool for a few seconds, arise, raise his pants, and return to where he was discovered wet.

Repeat the above steps 6 times. Do not reward or praise during this required practice. Use verbal instructions and graduated guidance, if necessary, fading them on each succeeding trial.

---

all times, yet firm in the expectation that the act must be performed. He does not argue, coax, threaten, cajole, or use excessive force. If the resident does resist, he pauses until the resident realizes that there is no intent to disturb him, but that the task must be accomplished. The following examples of resistive behavior may be encountered. Also described is the method used to gradually overcome the resident's resistance.

Resident Goes Limp

One of the most common forms of resistive behavior is passive resistance, i.e., the resident goes limp by slumping to the floor or hanging his arms listlessly at his side. The first rule in avoiding this problem is to always maintain physical contact with the resident. The trainer should stand slightly behind the resident with the trainer's right hand grasping the resident's shirt or dress midway between the shoulder blades. If the resident is known to be resistive, the trainer, as a precaution, should grasp the resident from the back in this fashion as soon as he is discovered wet and direct the resident to walk with gentle forward pressure. Whenever a specific movement is required of the resident, the trainer uses this back pressure to guide the resident either forward, sideward, bending, or erect. For example, the trainer would hand the resident the mop while holding on to the resident's clothing with his right hand. Throughout the task, the trainer continues to hold the resident's clothing so that he can lift him up if he starts to slump. After the resident has been lifted a few times, he generally will cease trying to go limp. As long as you can maintain a grip on the resident's clothing, you have a good deal of control over the resident.

Another frequent form of passive resistance is when the resident allows his hands to go limp, perhaps because most of the tasks in the Full Cleanliness Training require that the resident use his hands. The most effective way to avoid this problem is for the trainer to use graduated guidance to guide the resident's hands. The trainer should lean over and into the resident's back and bring his hands around so that they are resting on top of the resident's hands. By causing the resident to stoop over slightly, the trainer reduces the resident's irrelevant gross body movements. With the trainer's hands resting on top of the resident's hands the trainer can apply just enough pressure to guide the desired movements through task completion. As the resident begins moving his hands appropriately, the trainer reduces the guidance but maintains contact with the trainee's hands to reapply guidance should it be necessary.

Most of the resistance you will encounter during the Cleanliness Training will occur when the resident is requested to mop, probably because mopping is a new skill for him. Or, it may be resisted because the mopping involves more physical effort. For residents who are especially resistive or unmanageable, it is some-times advisable to have the resident wipe up his accident with a cloth rather than a mop. Similarly, for small children, a mop is too large and unwieldy; a cloth should be used. The resident should still fill a pail with water and disinfectant and use the cloth to wipe up.

When the resident becomes too unmanageable, the trainer should take the resident to his own bed where the resident should be required to lie in a prone position until his agitation has diminished. Once the resident has become quiescent, he should be required to return to the training area and to finish the remaining time of his Full Cleanliness Training.

Verbal Resistance

During the Cleanliness Training, a resident may try to dissuade the trainer by shouting. The trainer should reassure the resident, inform him once again of the need to clean up the accident, all in a neutral tone of voice, and continue to require that he go through Cleanliness Training.

Recording During Training

Daytime Toilet Training Checklist

The Daytime Toilet Training Checklist shown in Figure 6 serves two functions. First, it provides the trainer with a step-by-step guide of the complete training procedure. Second, it contains spaces for recording the resident's progress during training. A Checklist should be available for each resident each day. The trainer should check off or fill in each item as it is completed. Parts 1 and 2 are designed to aid the trainer in making all the necessary pre-training arrangements. Part 3 is to be used until the resident self-initiates his toileting. On Part 3 the trainer records the number of cups of fluid consumed at each half-hour toileting, the exact time of accidents, appropriate urinations, and the first self-initiation. All other boxes are checked or left blank where appropriate. Part 4 is used after the resident has self-initiated for the first time. Note that several of the blocks have instructions printed in bold type. These instructions indicate that a procedural change is to be made from the previous self-initiation. For example, on Step 3, the instructions *Give No Edible* after self-initiations 3, 5, 6, 8, and 9 are used in fading out the resident's dependence on being rewarded for toileting. Similarly, the progression of time intervals between dry-pants inspections is shown for each self-initiation in Step 9.

When Is the Resident's Training Complete?

After 9 self-initiated toiletings, the trainer terminates the resident's training. The resident is then scheduled for the Ward Maintenance Program.

General Psychological Effects of the Training Program

Concerns voiced about the training program include whether the training time each day might be too long, whether residents should be required to clean up their own accidents, and whether the residents were capable of understanding the purpose of training. None of these concerns are warranted. Most residents will find their training pleasant and are disappointed when it is completed. Residents who have finished training often attempt to reenter the training area. The reasons for this lie in the nature of the program itself. During the entire training period, the resident is the center of attention. He receives frequent social interaction from a trainer, and this attention is shared with only one or two other residents. In the beginning of training, the resident is rewarded every 5 minutes with a piece of candy or a treat if his pants are dry. The resident also receives physical guidance which is a pleasant experience for many residents. The resident receives a variety of flavorful beverages and edible treats, some of which are normally unavailable to him on the ward. The trainer smiles at him, caresses him, and talks to him. When viewed this way, it is easy to see why most residents look upon the training as a very pleasant and rewarding experience.

This positive attention toward the resident is continued during the post-training Maintenance Program, but there are additional benefits at that time for the resident. He can attend activities off the ward or trips outside the institution since he is now continent. Consequently, the artificially arranged concentration of pleasant events during the training period is followed by the naturally occurring pleasant events in the institution at large. A major reason for not allowing a resident to leave a ward situation is that the resident is either incontinent or a severe behavior problem. When a resident is dry, other residents and staff will generally begin interacting with him and including him in pleasurable activities.

The training program builds responsibility in the resident. Once the resident has been toilet trained he often appears more responsive in other areas so that teaching of other complex sets of behavior is often accomplished more rapidly.

At no other time during the resident's stay in the institution will he be under as much continuous observation as during the toilet training period. During training, the resident and the trainer spend hour after hour each day together in continuous interaction. This time is spent in the bathroom, a rather small space, so that most of the resident's behavior is seen by the trainer. Here we see another major benefit of the training program. The trainer will learn more about the resident's capabilities and desires during the few days of training than he would learn in several years of casual care. Trainers have reported that during training, they discovered that many residents functioned at a much higher level than they had ever imagined. For example, trainers have heard residents who were thought to be mute actually speaking a few words.

Occasional Problems in Training

Resident Has an Accident While on His Way to or from the Toilet

If the resident has an accident on his way to or from the toilet when (1) he has self-initiated, he should be given Full Cleanliness Training and Positive Practice Training; (2) he was prompted, he should be required to clean up the accident briefly and given Positive Practice Training until the next scheduled toileting period.

61

Figure 6   Daytime Toilet Training Checklist*

Check each item when completed.

Part 1

Check the following before beginning training:

✓ 1.   Did the residents begin receiving fluids one hour before starting training? (p. 44)

✓ 2.   Is the training area blocked off or is an alternate toilet available for other residents? (p. 28)

✓ 3.   Are the residents wearing the underpants and pants alarms? (p. 31)

Part 2

Are the materials listed below in the bathroom?

✓ 1.   Extra underpants with snaps attached

✓ 2.   Chairs

✓ 3.   Urine alerts placed in toilet bowls

✓ 4.   Small table

✓ 5.   Variety of fluids

✓ 6.   Edible treats

✓ 7.   Drinking glasses or cups marked with the residents' names

✓ 8.   Kitchen timer or pocket timer

✓ 9.   Clean cloths for wiping up accidents

✓ 10.   Daytime Toilet Training Checklist

Figure 6, continued

Part 3   Bladder Training Sequence
(See p. 44)

Start exactly on the half-hour, for example, 8:00 or 8:30

Starting Time **8:00**   Resident's Name **Sam T.**   Date **2/18/73**

Check under the appropriate item when completed. Repeat the following steps every half-hour until a self-initiation occurs.	8:00	8:30	9:00	9:30	10:00	10:30	11:00	11:30	12:00	12:30	1:00	1:30	2:00	2:30	3:00	3:30	4:00	4:30
1. Gave as much fluid as resident would drink while seated in his chair. Note number of cups of fluid consumed.	4	3		2		3	2	2		3	2	2						
a. Waited about 1 minute.	✓	✓		✓	✓	✓	✓	✓		✓	✓	✓						
2. Directed resident to toilet using the minimal possible prompt.	✓	✓	✓	✓	✓	✓	✓	✓	✓	✓	✓	✓						
3. Directed resident to pull his pants down using the minimal possible prompt.	✓	✓	✓	✓	✓	✓	✓	✓	✓	✓	✓	✓						
4. If resident voided:																		
a. Gave edibles and praise while he was seated, then directed him to stand.		✓	✓	✓	✓	✓	✓		✓	✓	✓	✓						
b. Directed resident to flush toilet using the minimal possible prompt.		✓	✓	✓	✓	✓	✓		✓	✓	✓	✓						
c. Note each time of voiding.		8:46	9:12	9:40	10:10	10:38	11:12		12:05	12:31	1:03	1:34						
5. If resident did not void within 20 minutes of drinking the fluids, directed him to stand.	✓								✓									
6. Directed resident to pull up his pants using the minimal possible prompt.	✓	✓	✓	✓	✓	✓	✓	✓	✓	✓	✓	✓						
7. Directed resident to his chair using the minimal possible prompt.	✓	✓	✓	✓	✓	✓	✓	✓	✓	✓	✓	✓						
8. Inspected resident for dry pants 5 minutes after he had been sitting and every 5 minutes thereafter; gave edible and praise if pants were dry.	✓	✓	✓	✓	✓	✓	✓	✓	✓	✓	✓	✓						
9. If accident occurred:																		
a. Gave Brief Cleanliness Training and Positive Practice. (p. 48)		✓		✓				✓										
b. Note exact time of occurrence.		8:51		9:39				11:51										

Continuously praise resident for being dry. When self-initiation occurs, start the self-initiation procedure. Give exact time of self-initiation **1:45**

Part 4   Self-Initiation Training (resident walks to toilet by himself)
(See p. 53)

Resident's Name **Sam T.**   Date **2/18/73**

Check under the appropriate item when completed.	Self-Initiation: 1	2	3	4	5	6	7	8	9	10	
1. Time self-initiation occurred.	1:45	2:15	2:33	2:47	3:01	3:14	3:18	3:53	4:21		
2. If resident had trouble lowering his pants, gave minimal prompt.	✓	✓									
3. If resident voided, gave edible and praise while seated, then allowed him to get up on his own, and gave minimal prompt to flush toilet.	✓	✓	Give no edible	✓	Give no edible	Give no edible	✓	Give no edible	Give no edible		
4. If resident did not void, allowed him to get up on his own.						✓					
5. If resident had trouble raising his pants, gave minimal prompt.	✓	✓	✓								
6. Moved resident's chair further from the toilet.	✓	✓	✓	✓	✓		✓	✓	✓		
7. Directed resident to his chair.	✓	✓	✓	✓	✓	✓	✓	✓	✓		
8. Gave resident fluids.	✓	✓	✓	✓	✓	Give no fluids	✓	✓	Give no fluids		
9. Inspected resident for dry pants at the appropriate time intervals; gave edible and praise if pants were dry.	Every 5 minutes ✓	Every 10 minutes ✓	Every 20 minutes ✓	Every 30 minutes ✓	Every 45 minutes ✓	Every 60 minutes ✓	Every 90 minutes ✓	Every 120 minutes ✓	Every 120 minutes ✓		
10. If accident occurred:											Discontinue Training; Begin Maintenance Program
a. Gave Full Cleanliness Training and Positive Practice.						✓					
b. Note exact time of occurrence.						3:25					

63

Resident Continues to Urinate
as He Arises from the Toilet

If a resident continues to urinate as he rises from the toilet, one of two things has probably happened: (1) either the trainer heard the urine alert and rewarded and started to prompt the resident to get up before he actually finished urinating, or (2) the resident has learned that urinating brings a reward but has not yet learned to remain seated until he is finished urinating. To eliminate this problem, reward the resident while he is still sitting on the toilet, and continue to praise him until he has stopped urinating. Then wait about 15 seconds before telling him to stand up. Cleanliness Training should not be given if the resident is still urinating as he arises from the toilet. Should the resident mistakenly try to rise while he is still urinating, the trainer should gently restrain him from standing.

Misdirected Urination

When sitting on the toilet bowl, a male resident may accidently urinate on his legs or on the floor rather than in the toilet. This problem is caused by an upward orientation of the penis and should not be considered as an accident. To solve this problem, the trainer should have the resident lean slightly forward, while seated on the toilet, causing the penis to be angled downward so that the stream of urine goes into the toilet (urine alert). Children often lean back if the toilet seat is adult-sized. To create a forward-leaning position, place a block of wood, cardboard box, or similar back support behind the child's back. This forward-leaning position has the additional benefit of allowing the resident to urinate and defecate more easily.

Refusal to Sit on the Toilet (Hyperactivity)

Some residents may refuse to remain seated on the toilet. This is especially true of young retarded children who are generally quite active. Refusal to sit for more than brief periods is also common among hyperactive residents or residents who consistently refuse to follow instructions. These residents find nothing rewarding about sitting on the toilet since in the past they often sat there for long periods of time without eliminating. Were they bladder trained, they would eliminate almost immediately and be able to leave the toilet. The requirement to sit on the toilet for long periods of time can become very aversive, since the resident cannot engage in other activities that he may find rewarding. The solution, then, is to make sitting on the toilet rewarding by immediately rewarding the resistive resident as soon as his buttocks make contact with the toilet seat.

Use graduated guidance to maintain this seated posture. Meanwhile, gradually stretch out the time between rewards so that the resident must sit for a second or two before receiving a reward, and then several seconds, and so forth, up to a minute or several minutes. Gradually fade out the scheduled rewards so that the resident will remain seated indefinitely without the need for continuous approval. When the resident urinates while sitting on the toilet, he will, of course, be rewarded immediately and allowed to stand. This shaping procedure builds up a positive association between the toilet and the receipt of an edible treat and praise. Should this hyperactivity be especially severe, do not include the hyperactive resident in a group training situation. Instead, defer his training for individual sessions so that the other residents in the group are not neglected. When the hyperactive resident will sit for several minutes, he can then be included in the group toilet training program. Even residents who are not hyperactive may attempt to rise when sitting on the toilet stool. This can be easily dealt with by using graduated guidance. The trainer places his hand on the resident's shoulder and gently guides him back on the toilet, exercising care to decrease the guidance as the resident realizes what is desired and discontinues even momentarily his attempt to stand. Otherwise, of course, the resident may interpret the forceful attempt at seating him as physical coercion and react emotionally.

Temper Tantrums (Refusal to Engage in Training)

Toilet training is an occasion in the resident's life when he must respond to social demands. It is not surprising, therefore, that a resident who has resisted socialization may respond to the training by having a temper tantrum. The problem is more common among children than adults. The resident may scream or cry when the trainer requires him to sit on his chair, lower or raise his pants, or sit on the toilet. Tantrums are usually only a problem in the first few hours of training before the resident realizes that he will be lavishly rewarded and praised. The guiding rule is that the trainer must not allow a tantrum to postpone or delay the training. The trainer should gently but firmly require that the resident perform each of the simple steps at the expected time. When it is time to perform a given act, such as approaching the toilet at the half-hour interval, the tantrum can be eliminated by using graduated guidance coupled with praise for performing the act. For example, if the resident begins shouting when required to arise from the chair and approach the toilet, use graduated guidance to gently, but firmly, move him forward. As soon as his shouting diminishes or stops even for an instant, immediately praise him, as long as you feel that he is making any effort to move forward as you are guiding him. Continue the praise up to the moment that physical resistance or total passivity occurs or when the shouting starts again. Do not coax, cajole, or nag during the tantrum; at most, repeat the verbal prompt in a neutral tone, "Johnny, go to the toilet." The same rules of ignoring the tantrum and praising cooperation also apply to tantrums during any of the other toileting acts. If objects have been disturbed during the tantrum, the trainer should require the resident to restore the object to its correct position after he completes the tantrum and is quiet. Each step in the training procedure should be conducted regardless of any tantrums. The resident will quickly learn that he cannot terminate the training by having a tantrum but that love and approval will be continuous if he does not have the tantrum.

Fondling the Genitals While Seated

The resident may begin to fondle his or her genitals during the initial phase of bladder training while sitting on the toilet. This may be disturbing to some staff members or to the trainers. It also interferes with bladder training in that the residents are too preoccupied to attempt to eliminate promptly. Discouraging genital stimulation at this time is, therefore, advisable. Fondling can be easily discouraged by distracting the resident. When he begins to fondle himself, the trainer should matter of factly call him by name and offer him an object to hold, such as a cup, to stop the fondling. He should not be given an item that absorbs his attention for long periods since this preoccupation will interfere with training just as fondling had. Should the resident express no interest in the object, the trainer should gain the resident's attention by briefly talking to him. The problem should, in any event, be only temporary since the toilet training procedure emphasizes immediate elimination upon sitting on the toilet, thereby minimizing the opportunity for fondling at that time. The problem exists primarily at the start of training when the resident is seated on the toilet with his pants lowered and has not yet learned to urinate immediately and to arise.

Refusal to Drink Fluids

To ensure that the trainee will drink a sufficient quantity of fluids during the training procedure, the trainer provides him with a wide selection of fluids to choose from as standard procedure (see Increased Consumption of Fluids, p. 34). If the resident still does not drink sufficient fluids, it is usually because he is in a strange situation, is not certain of the nature of the drink, is distracted by other events or thoughts, or that he is accustomed to drinking primarily while eating. Three procedures can be used to overcome these problems.

66

First, provide the solid edible treats used as the reward for being dry immediately prior to offering the drink. Peanuts or potato chips have an added advantage of stimulating drinking but any solid food given is beneficial. Second, touch the cup to the resident's lips so that he can taste the drink, thereby eliminating the problem of distraction by other events. Third, praise the resident immediately upon his accepting the fluid so that he realizes that drinking in these unaccustomed surroundings is sanctioned at this time.

Refusal to Eat the Candy or Edible Reward

The standard procedure for deciding what to use as a reward is to use candy or edibles that the residents like, give them a variety to choose from, and use bite-sized portions of the regular meal. If the resident is still refusing some of the edible reward, the reasons are usually the same as those outlined for the resident's reluctance to drink fluids. He is in a location where eating has not occurred previously, he may be distracted, and he may be unfamiliar with or forget the tastiness of the edible. The solution is similar. Place the edible reward into the resident's mouth such that he is certain to taste or sample the edible and hold it there for several seconds before concluding that he does not want it. For the bite-sized portions of his meal, at least, eager ingestion should result. Similarly, praise the resident as soon as he is seen to taste or bite into the food so that he realizes you approve of his eating in this situation.

Resident Does Not Initiate Toileting Without Being Prompted

Once the resident has been bladder trained, he will learn to approach the toilet without being prompted. If difficulties arise in obtaining this self-initiation, refer to the prompting-fading procedures described on page 38. The difficulty is usually caused by fading out the prompts too rapidly and will be solved by fading them out in the graduated sequence of reduced gestures listed in Table 2, p. 39. A problem that may arise is that the resident toilets once or twice without prompting but then reverts to the earlier stage of waiting for the trainer's prompt. This is caused by the understandable impatience of the trainer. Once the resident has self-initiated toileting, even once, no toilet-approach prompts should be given. Rather, the trainer must now wait for the resident to approach the toilet on his own initiative rather than prompt him every half-hour. If much time has elapsed since the last toileting, the trainer may become uneasy and deviate from the prescribed procedure by prompting the resident. This reintroduction of prompts is interpreted by the resident to mean that he should await prompts before toileting. The solution is to discontinue prompts totally after the first self-initiation. Do not become impatient since a resident may wait up to six hours and then self-initiate. Or he may well have three or four accidents at this time, but will quickly learn that his cleanliness is important (through the Full Cleanliness Training) and be remotivated to resume his unprompted toiletings. A period of "testing" sometimes arises at this transition; the resident allows himself to soil once or twice to test whether the trainer's expectations have indeed changed permanently.

The Physically Handicapped Resident Who Is Ambulatory

The physical capabilities necessary for self-initiation are ambulation, some sight, and motor control of at least one arm and hand (see p. 23). There are residents who meet these criteria, who nonetheless have associated physical handicaps that require special attention during the toilet training.

Unsteady Locomotion

Toilet training will present a special problem if a resident has difficulty in walking such as might occur with geriatric residents, paralysis or injury to one leg, vestibular dysfunction, or unsteadiness of gait for other reasons. This problem will not interfere appreciably with the training in the toilet area since the resident need only walk a few steps from the chair to the toilet bowl. After the first self-initiation, however, the resident must walk a longer distance and may be understandably reluctant to risk the danger of falling en route to the toilet from a distant day room. His slow progress also requires him to anticipate well in advance the need to urinate. Since these problems will continue during the post-training period, provide a railing along all walls and corridors that lead toward the toilet area. The increased mobility permitted by this railing will probably increase the resident's other activities as well.

Partial Disability of the Hands and Arms

Some profoundly retarded residents have some motor control of one hand, but the other hand may suffer from flaccid or spastic paralysis. These residents require special training to learn how to use the functional arm and hand to raise and lower their pants when toileting. As long as the resident has sufficient control to "hook" a finger or thumb over or under his waistband, he can be toilet trained. Use graduated guidance to teach the resident to pull first one side of the pants and then the other side in a continuously alternating fashion

68

using the functional hand in a "hooking" motion. This training should be given prior to toilet training.

Poor motor control of one or both hands may also cause difficulty for females in pulling their dresses up and out of the way when sitting down on the toilet. One solution is to provide a shorter dress such that the hand can reach under it more easily. If the hand-arm disability is too severe for this solution, vertically slit the lower back of the dress. The slit dress will automatically spread out and away from the toilet during the sitting position and will eliminate the need for the female resident to pull up her dress. Still another solution is to substitute culottes for the dress, thus removing the need for lifting the dress.

Deafness

Partial or nearly complete deafness is somewhat common among the profoundly retarded. The deafness creates problems for toilet training in that the resident cannot respond readily, if at all, to verbal praise, verbal prompts, or general verbal instructions. If the deafness is mild, the trainer should speak very loudly and face the resident who can then gain extra cues from the lip movements and facial expressions. If the deafness is more severe, the trainer should substitute and exaggerate the non-auditory modes of giving praise. When rewarding approval is given, the trainer should pat and hug the resident, smile very visibly, and nod his head repeatedly. Gross visible gestures such as pointing and tactual orientation, as used in graduated guidance, should be emphasized as the substitute for verbal instructions and prompts. Since the profoundly retarded person is often inattentive and unmotivated, considerable difficulty may exist in definitely determining whether a resident is deaf or whether he is inattentive. Consequently, the trainer should assume that the resident can hear at least partially unless definite evidence exists to the contrary. The trainers should, in such doubtful cases, speak loudly while praising or instructing the resident while still emphasizing the gestural, tactual, and visual factors noted above. Once trained, the resident will not have toileting problems because of his deafness, since the training produces unprompted toileting and the facial expressions of staff approval for dryness will readily serve as a motivator.

Blind, Nonambulatory (Wheelchair)

If the resident is blind or is confined to a wheelchair, assistance by a staff member is usually needed for the resident to toilet himself. Consequently, unprompted and unassisted toileting is not a reasonable objective and the training program should be limited to bladder training only. Follow the same procedure as for the ambulatory residents, except:

1. Lead the resident to the toilet bowl. Prompting and guiding to the toilet bowl are not used.

2. Omit the dressing and undressing requirements for the nonambulatory. For the blind, however, these skills are still reasonable objectives.

3. Omit the Cleanliness Training and Positive Practice if the resident has an accident but retain the usual omission of the 5-minute rewards for dry pants.

4. Terminate training when the resident has spent an entire training day (6 hours or more) with no accidents and with most eliminations occurring within 5 minutes after sitting on the toilet.

The bladder training procedure ensures that the resident will eliminate promptly upon being seated on the toilet by the attendants.

CHAPTER 6

THE MAINTENANCE PROGRAM

The resident now knows how to toilet himself. Under the intensive attention of the trainer, he has demonstrated that he can keep himself dry without the need for reminders. The problem now is to motivate the resident to use his newly acquired skill as a member of the institutional ward.

Ordinarily, motivation to be continent comes from several sources. Soiled or stained clothing results in social disapproval and it takes time and effort to clean up the accident. Incontinence interferes with established practices such as eating in a group. Unfortunately, the diagnosis of retardation and the fact of institutionalization probably have reduced these influences. Because the individual is known to have difficulty in learning, his incontinence is excused, and he is denied responsibility for his actions.

The Maintenance Program creates this motivation for the newly trained resident by changing the manner in which the staff views his incontinence. Figure 7 outlines the revised manner in which the staff reacts to the resident's continence or incontinence. First, staff approval for continence is arranged by scheduling several moments in the day when social approval is given for being dry. This is the Dry-Pants Inspection procedure (p. 73). Second, the resident now assumes responsibility for his incontinence. When he soils himself or his surroundings, he is required to correct the situation by cleaning himself, his clothing, and his surroundings through Full Cleanliness Training which was also used during the latter stage of training (p. 55). Third, the resident learns that incontinence interferes with his participation in basic ward functions, two of which are eating in the dining room and going to bed at night. Fourth, a "reminder" procedure, Positive Practice, is used to ensure that the resident has not forgotten his training. The Positive Practice procedure requires that the resident practice going to the toilet from different ward locations. This "reminder" is given only when an accident occurs and follows the Full Cleanliness Training.

The special motivating influences are gradually faded out once the resident shows himself to be sensitive to his appearance. The motivation to remain dry is then part of the resident's general

Figure 7   Daily Maintenance Procedure

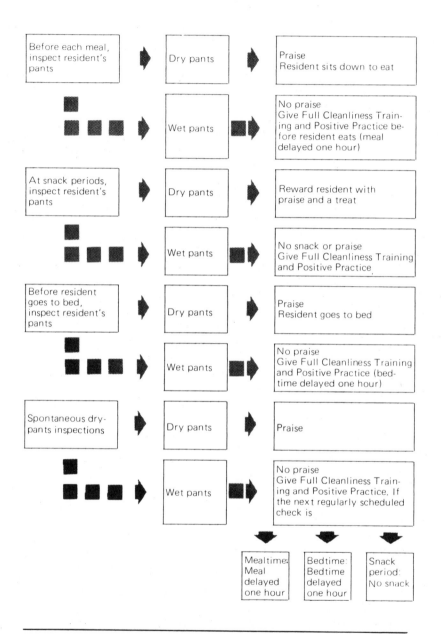

attitude and does not require the frequent scheduling of rewards and reminders that are outlined in Figure 7.

The first few days following training are the most critical for they establish the pattern for future behavior. The Maintenance Program is merely an extension of the training program so that the resident is not required to learn anything new.

Dry-Pants Inspection

Scheduling

A schedule of dry-pants inspections is used to reward the resident for staying dry. Inspections for dry pants were made every 5 minutes during the initial part of training but were then faded out to one inspection every 2 hours at the end of training. The Maintenance Program starts with a dry-pants inspection every 2 hours, thereby providing a gradual transition. Although it might seem adequate for the staff to inspect the residents for dry pants whenever they have a chance to do so, that practice will not be sustained over many days. Instead, a regular schedule of inspections is established with any spontaneous inspections by the staff welcomed and encouraged as supplements to the scheduled ones. To make the timing of the inspections convenient and natural to the staff and the resident, the inspection times occur when all residents are certain to be present, when staff supervision of some other activity ordinarily occurs, and when a natural association exists between the activity and being dry. The 3 meals and the time for retiring to bed at night fill these criteria. In addition, 2 snack periods are scheduled, one of them midway between breakfast and lunch and the other midway between lunch and supper. The inspection times might then be Breakfast at 7:30 a.m., Morning Snack at 9:30 a.m., Lunch at 11:30 a.m., Afternoon Snack at 2:00 p.m., Supper at 5:30 p.m., Bedtime at 8:00 p.m. This schedule provides 6 inspections per day, in addition to the spontaneous staff inspections (noted at bottom left of Figure 7).

Dry-Pants Inspection Procedure

The same Dry-Pants Inspection procedure used during the training program is used during the Maintenance Program—the resident is required to look at and feel the crotch region of his pants (see upper portion of Table 12). The mealtime dry-pants inspections should be made at the entrance to the residents' dining room. By inspecting the residents at the dining room entrance, the Maintenance Supervisor (see p. 75) will be easily reminded to inspect each resident as he enters, and the resident will quickly learn that he is to have dry clothing when eating. The bedtime dry-pants inspection should be made at the resident's bed before he has taken off his clothing. Again, from the inspection in their bedrooms by their beds, the residents will associate the need to be dry with retiring for the night. There is not a specific location where the between-meal dry-pants inspections are to be made. The residents can either be assembled at some location on the ward or the Maintenance Supervisor can walk through the ward and inspect the residents.

Table 12   Dry-Pants Inspections During Maintenance
(At Breakfast, Lunch, Dinner, the 2 Snack periods, and Bedtime)

---

1. Ask resident if he is dry.
2. Have resident feel and look at his pants.
3. If pants are dry:
    a. Resident should be praised ("John, you're a good boy, you have dry pants") and allowed to eat, sleep, or join the ward activity.
    b. At the snack period, give resident the snack in addition to praising him.
4. If pants are wet, have resident go through Full Cleanliness Training and Positive Practice.
    a. If accident is detected prior to a meal, resident's meal is delayed one hour.
    b. If accident is detected prior to a snack period, resident does not receive the snack.
    c. If accident is detected prior to bedtime, resident cannot go to bed for an hour.

If the resident's pants are dry when he is inspected he should be praised and either given a snack or allowed to continue an activity, i.e., to eat or retire for the night (see Figure 7). At the spontaneous dry-pants inspections, the resident should be praised when he is found in dry pants.

When the Resident Is Found Wet

During training the trainer's negative reaction to the resident's wet pants was to admonish him and to omit the edible treat at the next dry-pants inspection. The resident was also given Cleanliness Training (either Brief Cleanliness Training if he hadn't yet self-initiated or Full Cleanliness Training if he had self-initiated) and Positive Practice Training immediately following the accident. The trainer was able to provide an immediate reaction to the accident because

74

the pants alarm signaled the onset of the accident. Since the resident does not wear the pants alarm after training is completed, an accident will not usually be detected until the next scheduled dry-pants inspection. Thus, the Maintenance Supervisor should give Full Cleanliness Training and Positive Practice immediately following a dry-pants inspection to avoid further delaying a negative reaction to the accident. The Positive Practice Training should be repeated 6 times, each time from a different location on the ward. Full Cleanliness Training and Positive Practice at this time will result in a postponement of the resident's meal or bedtime since he will not have changed into dry pants until Full Cleanliness Training and Positive Practice are completed. His meal or bedtime should be postponed by one full hour so that he will readily learn that incontinence is totally incompatible with eating or retiring. For the same reason, when the resident is discovered wet at the between-meal dry-pants inspections, this extra snack should be omitted entirely (this omission is identical to that during the Dry-Pants Inspection procedure during training) and the resident given Full Cleanliness Training and Positive Practice.

If a resident is found in wet clothing during a spontaneous dry-pants inspection, Full Cleanliness Training and Positive Practice should of course be given and the Maintenance Supervisor should indicate his displeasure to the resident. At the regularly scheduled dry-pants inspection following the detected accident, the resident should be reminded that he had wet his pants earlier and: (1) if the inspection period is at mealtime or bedtime, the resident's meal or bedtime should be delayed for an hour, (2) if a snack period follows a detected accident, the Maintenance Supervisor should show the resident the snack but explain to him that he cannot have it because he had earlier wet his pants. This ensures that the resident will learn that the same social reactions and postponements will occur regardless of when his accidents occur (see Figure 7 and lower portion of Table 12). Otherwise, the resident may be rewarded after having soiled himself within the last half-hour.

Maintenance Supervisor

Certification of Proficiency

During the toilet training program the ward staff's involvement was slight, since only one or two individuals served as toilet trainers. In the Maintenance Program, however, the entire ward staff is involved. Each day the Ward Supervisor will designate a staff member as being responsible throughout his working day for conducting the Maintenance Program. This staff member will be designated as the Maintenance Supervisor for that work shift. Each member of the ward staff must be trained to serve as Maintenance Supervisors. The training should be conducted by a toilet trainer or some other staff member who is familiar with the Maintenance Program. Several staff members can be trained simultaneously by having them take turns making dry-pants inspections, giving Full Cleanliness Training, Positive Practice, recording, etc., all under the toilet trainer's supervision. Once a staff member has demonstrated that he can perform the duties of a Maintenance Supervisor, the toilet trainer will certify him as capable of conducting the daily Maintenance Program. The current list of certified Supervisors should be posted in a central area. If a staff member has difficulty learning the duties of a Maintenance Supervisor, he should continue to receive training; certification is postponed until those difficulties are overcome. Training should continue until all staff members are certified so that the resident will learn more quickly that all of the staff are consistently responsive to his new skill. When new staff are assigned to the ward, training in

---

Table 13   Duties of the Maintenance Supervisor

---

1.   To conduct the regularly scheduled dry-pants inspections and to indicate this by initialing the Daily Maintenance Record sheet (p. 78).

2.   To make frequent spontaneous dry-pants inspections throughout his shift.

3.   To conduct Full Cleanliness Training and Positive Practice when required.

4.   To ensure that the meal or bedtime of a soiled resident is postponed for one hour after the scheduled meal or bedtime.

5.   To ensure that the resident receives his postponed meal or retires for the night one hour after the accident is detected.

6.   To record the accidents that occurred during his shift on the Daily Maintenance Record sheet (p. 78).

7.   To ensure that the female residents are all wearing underpants.

8.   To notify his substitute should he become unavailable at any time.

9.   To ensure an adequate supply of fresh clothing for the residents.

10.   To ensure that mops, cloths, sponges, etc., are available for Full Cleanliness Training.

11.   To ensure that an adequate supply of edibles are available to use as rewards during the between-meal snack periods.

12.   To request that the ward staff inform him of any residents they find with wet pants.

13.   To discuss problems and trends of his work shift with the Maintenance Supervisor who precedes or succeeds him on a work shift.

---

the Maintenance procedure should be given immediately. Table 13 is a summary listing of the duties of the Maintenance Supervisor.

Scheduling

For each work shift, a staff member who has been certified to serve as a Maintenance Supervisor should be assigned as the Maintenance Supervisor for that work shift. These assignments should be rotated throughout the entire list of certified Supervisors, so that each attendant will serve as a Supervisor approximately the same number of times. Whenever possible, a second certified staff member should be assigned on each shift as the Assistant Maintenance Supervisor to substitute for the main Supervisor when he is unavoidably absent that day or at lunch or on a coffee break. When his duties permit, the Assistant Supervisor should assist the Maintenance Supervisor, for example, by helping give Full Cleanliness Training when more than one resident is found wet.

Non-Maintenance Duties

Initially, when few residents (one to three) are on the Maintenance Program, the Maintenance Supervisor will not be overly occupied with the Maintenance Program. As a result, he will be available to perform other duties provided that they do not interfere with the Maintenance Program. It is especially important that he be free of any responsibilities for approximately one hour after each regularly scheduled dry-pants inspection so that he will have time to give Full Cleanliness Training should it be necessary. When possible, the Maintenance Supervisor should be assigned duties that will not take him off the ward or that do not require completion by a certain time. He will then be free to give Full Cleanliness Training following a spontaneous dry-pants inspection thereby providing a more immediate negative reaction to the resident's incontinence.

When the number of residents in the Maintenance Program increases to 6, the non-toileting duties of the Maintenance Supervisor must be correspondingly decreased. This reduction in non-toileting duties is necessitated by the need for the Supervisor to increase the frequency of the spontaneous dry-pants inspections in order to avoid detecting several residents with wet pants at one time as may be the case should the Supervisor only check the residents at the regularly scheduled dry-pants inspections. The Supervisor should not be burdened with such duties as supervising mealtimes, dispensing medication, or leaving the ward on errands. When 10 residents are on the Maintenance Program, the Maintenance Supervisor must be freed from all other duties.

Number of Residents
on the Maintenance Program

Since residents can be trained rather rapidly, often in only a few days, care must be taken not to allow too many residents at once on the Maintenance Program. All residents will "test" the Maintenance Program during their first days on Maintenance (i.e., the resident will try to discover if all the staff members have the same reactions to his accidents) thereby requiring the ward staff serving as Maintenance Supervisors to give several trials of Full Cleanliness Training per resident. If more than 10 residents are on Maintenance, the Maintenance Supervisors can become overwhelmed and be unable to do an adequate job of conducting Full Cleanliness Training should several residents be detected with wet pants at one time. The trainer should be instructed not to train additional residents until 10 or fewer are on the Maintenance Program.

Recording

The Daily Maintenance Record

The Daily Maintenance Record shown in Figure 8 contains the necessary information for conducting the Maintenance Program. The form shows: (1) which certified staff members have been assigned as Maintenance Supervisors, (2) the Daily Dry-Pants Inspection Record with spaces for the Maintenance Supervisor to initial at the completion of each of the 6 inspections, and (3) the detailed Daily Accident Chart. The assignment of Maintenance Supervisors should be made one week in advance on each pre-dated Daily Maintenance Record sheet. The form should be displayed in a central location thereby providing easy accessibility when recordings are to be made. The main focus of the Maintenance Program is on frequent dry-pants inspections since these are necessary if the newly trained residents are to remain continent. The Daily Dry-Pants Inspection shown at the upper portion of Figure 8 ensures that the regularly scheduled dry-pants inspections are carried out. The Maintenance Supervisor initials in the appropriate space after he finishes the inspections. The Daily Dry-Pants Inspection Record has several functions. First, it stresses accountability on the part of the Maintenance Supervisor ensuring that the inspections will be made. The Ward Supervisor can provide direct supervision of the inspections and will know who to contact should a procedural deviation occur. Second, an omitted inspection will be readily detected and can be immediately rescheduled. Third, the determination that inspections have been omitted can partially explain why accidents may be persisting. Finally, the Maintenance Supervisor will be providing his supervisors with tangible evidence that he is performing his duties. This introduces objectivity when his job performance is evaluated by his supervisor. The Daily Dry-Pants Inspection Record is reviewed each day by the Ward Supervisor.

Figure 8   Daily Maintenance Record*

Date __2/24/73__

Assigned Supervisors:
Morning Maintenance Supervisor __Jim Andrews__
Morning Asst. Maintenance Supervisor __Alice Jones__
Afternoon Maintenance Supervisor __Bill Lane__
Afternoon Asst. Maintenance Supervisor __Sarah Smith__

Daily Dry-Pants Inspection Record

Supervisor's initials when completed	Before breakfast check	Mid-morning snack check	Before lunch check	Mid-afternoon snack check	Before supper check	Before bed check
	J.A.	J.A.	J.A.	B1	B1	B1

Daily Accident Chart
(If an accident is unavoidable, place an asterisk beside the resident's name)

Resident's name	Time found wet	Starting time of Full Cleanliness Training and Positive Practice	Meal delayed	Bedtime delayed	Snack missed	Supervisor's initials when completed
Jimmy T.	6:45	6:50	✓			J.A.
David K.	9:30	9:35			✓	J.A.
Sam T.	11:30	11:35	✓			J.A.
Bruce Y.	11:30	11:35	✓			a.j.
Carl D.	5:05	5:05	✓			B1
Eddie P.	7:13	7:15		✓		B1
George A.*	7:21	Diarrhea — no Cleanliness Training or Positive Practice given				B1

The Daily Accident Chart, shown in the lower portion of Figure 8, is used to record accidents discovered at either the regularly scheduled or spontaneous dry-pants inspections. The following items are recorded: the resident's name, the time the accident was discovered, the giving of Full Cleanliness Training and Positive Practice, the disposition of the accident (meal, bedtime, or snack delayed), and the Maintenance Supervisor's initials. Since these recordings are made each time a resident is found wet, a resident may be listed several times on the Daily Accident Chart. Although the regularly scheduled dry-pants inspections are only made on residents in the Maintenance Program, the names of any other residents discovered wet should also be recorded. Since these residents are not on Maintenance, the only information recorded is their names and the times at which they were detected in wet pants. If the accident was unavoidable (see p. 85), place an asterisk (*) beside the resident's name.

Monthly Daytime Accident Chart

At the end of the day after the residents have retired for the night, the Maintenance Supervisor on the second work shift (p.m. or late afternoon) records each resident's daily number of accidents from the Daily Accident Chart onto the Monthly Daytime Accident Chart illustrated in Figure 9. The names of all the ward residents should be filled in at the beginning of the month. As residents are transferred to the ward, their names should be added under the special heading at the lower left-hand portion of the Monthly Daytime Accident Chart.

Figure 9 Monthly Daytime Accident Chart*

Month of __March 1973__

Instructions:

1. Fill in the names of all the ward residents at the beginning of the month.
2. Under the appropriate day record the number of accidents each resident had on that day. If none were detected, record a zero.
3. Place a capital *T* on the days the resident receives training.
4. Place a capital *M* on the day the resident enters the Maintenance Program.
5. Do not record accidents that are marked with an asterisk as unavoidable on the Daily Maintenance Record.

Day

Resident's Name	1	2	3	4	5	6	7	8	9	10	11	12	13	14	15	16	17	18	19	20	21	22	23	24	25	26	27	28	29	30	31	Total accidents for the month
Jimmy T. (M)	0	0	0	0	0	0	0	0	0	0	0	0	0	0	0	0	0	0	0	0	0	0	0	0	0	0	0	0	0	0	0	0
Billy G. (M)	0	1	0	0	0	0	0	0	1	1	0	0	0	1	0	0	0	0	0	0	0	0	1	0	0	0	0	0	0	0	0	5
Eddie P.	T	T	T	0	0	0	0	0	0	2	0	0	0	1	1	1	0	0	0	0	0	0	1	0	0	0	0	0	0	0	0	7
David K. (M)	1	1	0	0	0	0	0	0	0	0	0	0	0	0	0	0	0	0	0	0	0	0	0	0	0	0	0	0	0	0	0	2
Sam T. (M)	2	1	1	1	1	0	0	0	0	0	1	0	0	0	0	0	0	0	1	0	0	0	0	0	0	0	0	0	0	0	0	8
John B.	5	6	4	3	8	4	3	5	7	4	4	T	T	T	T	T	2	2	0	0	0	0	0	0	0	0	0	0	0	0	0	58
George A.	6	7	4	8	4	5	7	6	9	T	T	T	8	1	2	2	1	0	0	0	0	1	0	0	0	0	0	0	0	0	0	63
Bruce Y.	5	T	T	8	0	0	0	0	0	0	0	0	0	0	0	0	0	0	0	0	2	0	0	0	0	0	0	0	0	1	0	8
Carl D.	8	0	0	1	0	0	0	1	1	1	0	0	0	1	0	0	0	0	1	0	0	0	0	0	0	0	0	0	0	1	0	9
Ronnie G.	6	5	7	7	8	6	7	5	5	10	7	5	6	6	6	9	5	7	5	7	8	T	T	T	T	T	7	0	0	0	0	138

Residents transferred to ward since 1st of month	1	2	3	4	5	6	7	8	9	10	11	12	13	14	15	16	17	18	19	20	21	22	23	24	25	26	27	28	29	30	31	Total accidents for the month
Art M.																				7	6	8	8	5	4	6	T	T	7	0	0	45
Mack W.																								7	7	6	5	8	T	T		33

The Monthly Daytime Accident Chart provides the following useful and necessary information:

1. It allows determination of when to end the resident's Maintenance Program, since the resident must remain continent for 2 weeks before he is discontinued from Maintenance (see Termination of the Maintenance Program, p. 86). This is especially helpful since the date various residents are placed in the Maintenance Program will vary according to when they finish their training.

2. It provides monthly progress reports of the degree of ward continence which can then be circulated to concerned hospital administrators (see p. 89).

3. Residents who are having difficulty remaining continent will be immediately detected so that positive action can be taken (see Continued Accidents During Maintenance, p. 82).

Accidents

Accidents During Mealtimes and Programmed Activities

When an accident occurs during a meal or scheduled activity, immediately terminate the resident's participation in that activity. For example, if the resident has an accident while eating, he should complete his meal only after he has gone through the Full Cleanliness Training and Positive Practice Training. The same applies to accidents occurring during any scheduled on- or off-ward activity. For example, if the resident has an accident during a walk outside, he should be immediately returned to the ward and required to complete Full Cleanliness Training and Positive Practice. Usually, the resident will have accidents when no staff member is present, so that the majority of accidents will be detected at the spontaneous or regularly scheduled dry-pants inspections.

On wards where numerous daily activities are programmed, few residents will have accidents during the Maintenance Program, since there are many incentives for the resident to remain dry and soiling will result in a postponement of these activities. If a ward is primarily custodial, however, the staff is relying on dry-pants inspections alone to deter wetting. If there are not a number of activities available for the residents, you should seriously consider developing these programs prior to initiating the toilet training program. Following the training, the staff will have more time to conduct educational and recreational programs, since the residents will now be continent and the staff will no longer have to spend time in such activities as changing soiled clothing, housekeeping, and directing toileting.

Intentional Wetting

When a resident has an accident during an activity, his participation in that activity should be terminated and he should be required to engage in Full Cleanliness Training and Positive Practice. There are rare occasions when a resident is observed to wet purposefully in order to escape a situation he perceives as stressful. An example is wetting repeatedly during a scheduled language training class. When a resident repeatedly wets during one particular activity but does not at other times, it can be assumed that he perceives that activity as more stressful than Full Cleanliness Training and Positive Practice. To eliminate this problem, the resident should be required to complete the activity even when he has wet. When the activity is finished, the resident can then be given Full Cleanliness Training and Positive Practice. Once the resident learns that he cannot terminate his participation in the activity by wetting, he will cease having accidents during that activity.

Continued Accidents During Maintenance

Residents will usually have some accidents during their first weeks on the Maintenance Program. This is often because the resident is "testing" the staff's reactions to his accident. If the Maintenance Program is conducted consistently, accidents soon stop. Several factors can account for a continuation of accidents. The various procedures should be reread closely to ensure that they have been properly conducted. A few of the more common reasons for post-training accidents are reviewed below.

Failure to Properly Fade Out Dry-Pants Inspections
During Training

Wettings may continue during Maintenance if dry-pants inspections were not properly faded from every 5 minutes to every 2 hours during training since the resident's schedule of rewards was thinned too abruptly. This problem can be solved by scheduling more frequent dry-pants inspections and then increasing the time period between inspections as follows:

1. Dry-pants inspections should be made every 15 minutes the first day.
2. After the resident has remained dry for one day when inspected every 15 minutes, 30-minute dry pants inspections should be made the next day.
3. After the resident has remained dry one day when inspected every 30 minutes, one-hour dry pants inspections should be made the next day.
4. After the resident has remained dry one day when inspected every hour, the regular Maintenance Program (6 inspections) is begun on the next day.

Failure to Conduct Full Cleanliness Training Properly

Generally, three factors can significantly reduce effectiveness of Full Cleanliness Training. The first is inadvertent social attention by the Maintenance Supervisor. When the Supervisor does not deliver instructions in a neutral tone or when he speaks unnecessarily to the resident during Full Cleanliness Training, he provides the resident with social pleasantries for being incontinent. This positive interaction often confuses the resident since the Supervisor is not showing the slightest displeasure that the resident is incontinent. If the resident's interactions with the staff are limited, he may, in rare instances, begin soiling himself in order to receive the positive attention he has experienced during Full Cleanliness Training.

A second factor is conducting the Full Cleanliness Training for less than the specified 30-minute period. The Full Cleanliness Training constitutes a period of general instruction in the importance of remaining continent. In order for this instruction to be effective, sufficient time must be allowed (30 minutes) so that the resident can be adequately instructed in all phases of cleaning up (p. 55).

A third factor which reduces the effectiveness of Full Cleanliness Training occurs when the Maintenance Supervisor provides physical rather than graduated guidance. When only physical guidance is given, the resident remains passive and never learns to become responsible for his accidents. This dependence on the Supervisor can extend into other areas of the resident's toileting behavior since the resident may reason that his toileting is actually the responsibility of others rather than only himself.

Failure to Delay Meals or Snacks Following an Accident

A few wards have reported their residents were urinating in their pants soon after receiving a snack or eating a meal. The residents had learned that they could receive their snacks and meals by remaining dry for only 30 minutes prior to the inspection periods. They could wet at any other time and while required to receive Full Cleanliness Training and Positive Practice, they would not miss snacks or have their meals delayed. The solution to this problem, as stated on p. 73, is to postpone the meal or snack if the resident wet himself at any time since the last meal or snack.

Too Many Residents on the Maintenance Program at One Time

For a discussion of this problem and its solution, see p. 78.

Too Few Spontaneous Dry-Pants Inspections

This problem is especially troublesome when there are many residents on the Maintenance Program. Maintenance Supervisors should make frequent spontaneous inspections (see p. 73) of the resident's clothing to provide more immediate feedback to the resident that he should avoid soiling himself. Spontaneous dry-pants inspections allow the Full Cleanliness Training to be distributed more evenly in time so that the Supervisor does not have to conduct Full Cleanliness Training for several residents at the same time after a scheduled dry-pants inspection.

Termination of Training Before the Resident Began Toileting Himself

This problem occurs when the toilet trainer has inadvertently continued to prompt the resident to approach the toilet stool. For example, during the resident's self-initiation training the trainer may be unconsciously providing some sort of small gesture which the resident interprets as a signal (prompt) that he should toilet himself. Throughout the self-initiation training the resident continued to rely on the trainer to "tell" him when to toilet himself. Once the resident is placed on the Maintenance Program he will begin having accidents since he has never really toileted himself without prompting. When this problem is suspected, the resident should be placed in the toilet training program a second time. Before he again enters the Maintenance Program, special attention should be given to ensure that he is actually initiating his own toileting without prompts.

Possible Problems
During the Maintenance Program

Resident Does Not Toilet Without Notifying Staff

An occasional problem after training is that the resident will not go to the toilet unless he first tells a staff member by word or gesture that he wishes to toilet or has just toileted. This originates from the pleasant experience that the resident had during training when immediate reward was given for toileting. The program was designed to eliminate this problem of continuing notification by (1) eliminating the prompts during training, (2) gradually reducing the rewards after each toileting, and (3) rewarding the resident for being dry rather than the act of toileting. When this problem exists, the cause is likely to be one or more of the following: (1) prompts were not eliminated during training, (2) the reward for each toileting was not terminated at the end of training, (3) the dry-pants inspections during Maintenance were not being conducted properly, (4) the ward staff continued to praise the resident after training for the act of toileting, or (5) after Maintenance, the ward routine provided so few opportunities for staff attention that the resident continued notification as a means of getting staff attention.

Resident Hides His Wet Pants

The detection of accidents relies on visible evidence of wet pants. Although rarely done, a resident may try to avoid detection by removing his soiled pants. This problem and its solution are illustrated in the following example of a 45-year-old profoundly retarded man. William had been successfully toilet trained and was on the Maintenance Program. When William had an accident, however, he would take off his wet pants and hide them. He then removed dry pants from another resident. Only after the ward staff discovered the hidden wet pants, did they realize that William was still having accidents. The staff knew that he understood the purpose of Maintenance, since he made sure that he had dry pants when the regularly scheduled dry-pants inspections were made. The staff decided to increase the frequency of William's dry-pants inspections by checking him once an hour. During the first few days, he was discovered with wet pants on several occasions and given Full Cleanliness Training and Positive Practice each time. At the end of a week, William was dry at each of the hourly checks. The Maintenance Supervisor praised him at the hourly checks for having dry pants. William was then included in the regular Maintenance schedule of 6 checks per day.

Restrictive Clothing

Tight fitting clothing can be a source of post-training accidents. During the Maintenance Program, male residents should not be dressed in pants that have zippers, snaps, or a belt since these items interfere with the resident's pulling his pants down. Rather, male residents should wear loose fitting trousers with elastic waistbands until their independent toileting behavior has been well established. Once they have remained dry over an extended period, they can be given training in buttoning, snapping, zipping, and working with belts (Bensberg, 1965). A female resident's clothing can hamper her toileting when: (1) her underpants are too tight, (2) her dress is straight rather than full, or (3) she wears outer pants rather than a dress. Female residents should wear loose fitting dresses and underpants until their toileting behavior has been satisfactorily maintained. Then the women, like the men, can be taught to dress and undress themselves in a wider variety of clothing. Parents of a retarded female child should sacrifice style for convenience until their child has demonstrated that she can toilet herself and has received training in dressing in tighter fitting clothing such as leotards.

Off-Ward Accidents

When a resident remains continent while on the ward, but has accidents outdoors or in other areas, the problem is that he does not have access to a toilet or does not know how to obtain this access. This problem is understandably frequent when a resident is totally nonverbal or the attendant staff is unfamiliar with his gestural language. The solutions are to show residents where the toilets are in new situations, to leave access doors to the toilets unlocked when possible, and to provide a toileting opportunity before taking residents to an unfamiliar situation or one where no toilet is available.

Unavoidable Accidents

If a resident has a virus or an intestinal infection or disorder, any accidents should be considered unavoidable. Similarly, if a resident has an accident because he is in a situation where toileting is impossible or difficult, such as an extended bus trip, this accident should be considered unavoidable. *Unavoidable accidents should not result in Full Cleanliness Training or Positive Practice.*

Termination of the Maintenance Program

The criterion for terminating the Maintenance Program is that the resident has not had a single accident for 2 weeks, as determined from the Monthly Daytime Accident Chart (see Figure 9, p. 80). Unavoidable accidents indicated by an asterisk on that chart should not be counted in making this decision to terminate the program. Once the resident is no longer in the Maintenance Program, his accidents should be treated the same as the rare accidents of other continent residents who might not have received training. This treatment is described in the following section.

Normal Ward Reaction to Accidents

Once the resident has completed training and the Maintenance Program, he should not be returned to a ward situation which was responsible for the original problem of incontinence. Recall that part of the original problem was that the profoundly retarded person required more than normal social attention to desired behaviors in order to be motivated to engage in those behaviors. Therefore, the normal ward reaction to accidents should be changed such that the resident will continue his newly acquired responsibility for his own toileting. The normal ward reaction to the resident's accidents should now be the same as was used for accidents during the toilet training phase when the resident had not yet learned to control his toileting but where the beginnings of individual responsibility were established. Specifically, the resident should (1) clean up any soiling or puddle caused by the accident, (2) obtain fresh clothing to replace the soiled clothing, (3) wipe himself off to the limited extent needed to be clean again. No Positive Practice, washing of clothing, cleaning of the general ward area, or extensive self-bathing is needed at this time—only simple correction of the accident. Nor are special mid-meal inspection periods necessary. The usual approval that is given when a resident participates in pleasurable ward activities should be sufficient as an indirect reward for being continent. All residents on the ward should be included in this Normal Ward Procedure, including those that will not receive training since they have very infrequent accidents. For residents who are scheduled to be toilet trained soon, the application of this Normal Ward Procedure will facilitate training. This simple correction procedure should be conducted by all ward staff except the Maintenance Supervisor.

He will be sufficiently occupied by the intensive Maintenance Program duties and should be constantly attending to the residents who have just completed training. The general ward staff should routinely attend to the appearance of the residents during the conduct of all activities and require the simple correction procedure whenever a resident is incontinent.

CHAPTER 7

ENSURING ADMINISTRATIVE SUPPORT

As with most successful programs, one individual should take ultimate responsibility for the program. In the toilet training program, this individual should be the Ward Supervisor or Program Director who then functions as the Toilet Training Director or Coordinator. The duties of the Toilet Training Coordinator are summarized in Table 14.

Table 14   Duties of the Toilet Training Coordinator (Director)

---

1. To supervise the Training and Maintenance Programs.
2. To keep records, summarize these records, and forward them to the Institutional Director.
3. To evaluate the performance of the toilet trainers and the Maintenance Supervisors on their annual proficiency reports.
4. To make daily assignments of attendants as Maintenance Supervisors.
5. To review the Daily Maintenance Record sheet to ensure that all dry-pants inspections and accidents have been properly recorded.

The Program Director must gain the support of the Institutional Director. The first step in gaining this administrative support is to acquaint the Director with all the problems associated with institutional incontinence. Table 15 lists some of these problems and may be used by the Program Director in discussing the initiation of the program with the Institutional Director.

After the Institutional Director has indicated that a training program to eliminate incontinence is warranted, the extent of the institution's involvement in the program should be explained by presenting the Director with a list of institutional practices required in order to establish the training program. Table 16 lists these practices and may be used as a guide for discussion. Once the Director agrees to these practices, the program can be instituted. The Institutional Director should then notify the ward staff, in person or in writing, of his desire to support the program.

Table 15   The Effects of Incontinence on Residents, Staff, and the Institution*

Extent of the problem: _____ percent of the residents are incontinent (have more than one accident per week).

1. Incontinence represents a health hazard to residents and staff. Incontinence can result in chronic intestinal infestations by parasites (whipworms) or in epidemic bacterial infections such as shigella.

2. Incontinence is associated with serious maladaptive behaviors such as coprophagy (feces eating), feces smearing, and stripping.

3. Besides being unsanitary, incontinence produces unpleasant odors for residents, staff, and visitors.

4. Incontinence requires more laundry resulting in added expense.

5. Incontinence discourages discharge to home or the community.

6. Incontinence prevents on- and off-ward educational and recreational activities.

7. Incontinence requires additional ward personnel for administering to the toileting needs of the residents. These additional personnel are typically involved in cleaning up the residents and taking them frequently to the toilet.

8. Incontinence may require the addition of janitorial staff whose sole function is housekeeping activities.

9. Incontinence shows that the residents have not been taught to function independently even in the basic self-care skills.

After initiating the program, the Toilet Training Coordinator (Program Director) must provide the Institutional Director with feedback on the status of the program in order to ensure the Director's continued support and interest. One of the Coordinator's important functions is to provide the Institutional Director with a monthly progress report illustrated in Figure 10, the Monthly Daytime Toilet Training Summary. It furnishes the information of most interest to the Director, namely, the percent of the residents who are continent, the percent who are infrequently or regularly incontinent, and the percent these figures changed from the previous month. The information for filling out the Monthly Daytime Toilet Training Summary is from the Monthly Daytime Accident Chart (Figure 9, p. 80). The Coordinator should include only those residents who have resided on the ward during the entire previous and current months in calculating the total number of residents on the ward. Otherwise, the transfer of incontinent residents to the ward will inflate the percent of residents incontinent even though the residents who have received training are remaining dry. The number of accidents that each resident had per day can be obtained by dividing the number of days in the month (less the number of days the resident spent in training) into the number of accidents the

---

Table 16   Institutional Practices Needed to Establish the Rapid Toilet Training Program*

---

1. One or 2 staff members must be assigned full time as trainers. The time required for them to conduct training should be calculated as one week per 2 residents.

2. All the ward staff on the morning and afternoon work shifts must participate as Maintenance Supervisors. One staff member must be assigned full time on each work shift. The duties of the Maintenance Supervisor should be included in the attendants' job descriptions. Their performance as Maintenance Supervisors should be used as one of the bases for evaluating their job proficiencies.

3. The Ward Supervisor and/or Program Director must have responsibility for the training program. He must allocate his time to supervise the training program, to compile reports on the program's progress, and to forward these reports to his supervisors.

4. The Institutional Director should provide the Ward Supervisor with feedback on his satisfaction or dissatisfaction with the progress of the toilet training program.

5. The ward physician must give physical examinations to all residents who are to receive training.

6. The institution's dietary personnel must agree to cooperate in adjusting the residents' meal schedules when necessary.

7. The following training equipment and supplies must be provided:
    a. A variety of rewards, consisting of fluids and edibles
    b. Appropriate clothing, for example, underwear, trousers with elastic waistbands, dresses, culottes
    c. Toileting signal apparatuses
    d. Portable toilets if necessary
    e. Movable partitions if necessary

---

resident had during the month. Residents averaging less than one accident per day are considered infrequently incontinent; those averaging more than one accident per day are considered regularly incontinent. The percent of regularly incontinent residents is calculated by dividing the total number of residents on the ward into the number of regularly incontinent residents, multiplied by 100. The percent of infrequently incontinent residents is calculated by dividing the total number of residents on the ward into the number of infrequently incontinent residents, multiplied by 100. Similarly, the percent of residents continent is calculated in the above manner. The three percentages should add up to 100 percent. Percent change for each category is determined by subtracting the figure for the current month from the previous month's figure.

At the lower portion of the Summary sheet are spaces for the comments of the Toilet Training Coordinator and the Institutional Director. The Institutional Director should route the Monthly Daytime Toilet Training Summary back to the ward so that it can be displayed in a conspicuous place. The Institutional Director's comments will serve as a continuing reminder to the ward staff that he is concerned with the success of the program.

Figure 10   Monthly Daytime Toilet Training Summary*

Ward _____**1**_____

Monthly report of _____**March**_____

	This month	Last month	Percent change
Percent of residents continent	10	0	+ 10
Percent of residents infrequently incontinent[1]	60	0	+ 60
Percent of residents regularly incontinent[2]	30	100	- 70

Toilet Training Coordinator's signature   *Edward Simpson*

Comments: *The program is going very smoothly. We expect to eliminate all regular incontinence by the end of april.*

Institutional Director's signature _____ *James Cox* _____

Comments: *The program looks very good. Please convey my congratulations to the staff. Keep up the good work!*

Routing: Institutional Director and return

[1] Residents averaging less than one accident per day

[2] Residents averaging more than one accident per day

Ensuring Ward Staff Cooperation and Support

The entire ward staff and their supervisor should read and thoroughly discuss this manual before training begins. The Toilet Training Coordinator (Supervisor) should be assured that everyone understands the rationale and purpose of the Training and Maintenance Programs and that everyone has agreed to follow the specified guidelines. One method of detecting unvoiced doubts is for the Supervisor to ask each staff member individually to state whether he understands the program well enough to participate. This question is best raised in a group meeting so that the Supervisor's clarification will also remove the doubts and questions of other staff members. During the Training and Maintenance Programs, the trainers and staff should observe each other, and thereby learn how their individual performances might be improved. The Ward Supervisor should remind the staff that their performance in conducting the program will be seriously considered in the formal evaluations that may be required by the institution on either a regular basis or for promotions, reclassifications, or salary increases. This information should be announced to the staff members by all supervisors who have the formal responsibility for conducting evaluation of staff.

CHAPTER 8

TOILET TRAINING OTHER POPULATIONS

The Mentally Ill

This toilet training program can also be used to toilet train the mentally ill. The incontinence of the mentally ill is amost always a problem of motivation. Since the toilet training program is designed to overcome problems of motivation, essentially the same toilet training program is employed for the mentally ill as for the retarded.

The main difference is that verbal instruction is used almost exclusively rather than physical prompting since the mentally ill usually have adequate intellectual resources. A second difference is that the mentally ill patient almost always has already learned how to toilet himself, and therefore the need for the acquisition portion of the program is minimized. Thus bladder training is usually accomplished within a day. However, the patient should go through the entire program from the beginning since expectations should not be placed on him until he has demonstrated by self-initiating that he knows how to toilet himself.

The Geriatric Patient

Elderly patients have been continent in the past, but have now become incontinent. They now have physical problems that make it difficult for them to toilet themselves. Recent studies have shown, however, that eighty percent of incontinent geriatric patients are physically capable of controlling their bladders, and most of them are motivated to be continent. Because of their physical infirmities, the elderly patients require additional motivation and encouragement to engage in the various toileting behaviors that require more effort with advancing age.

Before instituting a toilet training program for the elderly, it is imperative that the patients receive a thorough physical examination by a urologist or a physician specializing in the problems of the aged. It is also important to have the physician determine how much activity the patient can perform. If the patient has the necessary musculature to control his bladder and is capable of performing some physical activity, then toilet training can be given. Many physicians feel that self-toileting by the elderly is beneficial to their over-all mental and physical condition even if extra effort is needed.

The training program for the elderly differs from that given the retarded in two ways. First, the training is given for no more than two or three hours each day. Second, the Full Cleanliness Training procedure is not given since the patient is usually incapable of cleaning up extensively. The patient should be required to correct the effects of his accident to the extent his physical condition permits.

Nonambulatory Patients

The bladder training program should be instituted for the non-ambulatory mentally ill and geriatric patients. The patient should be brought a bedpan if he is bedridden, or transported to the toilet in a wheelchair if he is capable of sitting. This should be done on a regular basis and the patient rewarded for eliminating. The general procedure is similar to that described for the nonambulatory retard-ate (see p. 69).

Home Training

Parents whose retarded child lives at home can conduct this toilet training program.

The major differences in the program when it is used in the home are:

1. It is not necessary to use the pants alarm or urine alert; detection of eliminations is not a problem since only one individual is being trained. However, you may wish to consider using the blue litmus paper (see p. 31). If the child is small enough for a potty chair, any commercially available potty chair can be used.

2. The full 30 minutes of Cleanliness Training may be unneces-sary. The simple correction of an accident (Brief Cleanliness Training), the visible displeasure of the parent, and Positive Practice, all completed within 10-15 minutes, are usually suffi-cient to discourage accidents.

If the child attends a training center or a special educa-tion class, home toilet training efforts should be coordinated with the teacher or staff to ensure a consistent approach to the child's toileting behavior. It is desirable for the teacher to also read this manual. The actual training should be done at home, but once train-ing has been completed, the parents should accompany their child to the training center or school to ensure that the child knows the location of the toilet. The teacher should be encouraged to check the child for dry pants periodically throughout the day. With both the parents and the teacher providing rewards for continence and displeasure for accidents during the Maintenance Program, the child should remain continent both in the home and at the training center.

CHAPTER 9

PROBLEM IDENTIFICATION:
A SELF-TEST FOR DAYTIME TRAINING

The following test will remind the training personnel of the principal procedures in the training program. Only those procedures are listed that are known to cause serious problems if omitted or conducted improperly.

This test will serve as a summary review. The test answers will (1) suggest what to do if problems arise in the program by calling attention to omitted procedural details and (2) serve as a reminder of what sections of the manual should be read again. When a problem arises in the program, the trainer and Supervisor should use this self-test as a method of discovering what procedural deviation caused the problem.

In addition, this self-test can be used before starting to train the first resident as a means of becoming alert to the most critical procedures. Then the questions should be answered a second time after the first day of training by a new trainer, then again after the first resident has been completely trained. This anticipation of problems will help to prevent them.

In answering each question, mark:

Not Sure if you are not certain of what was actually done,

Definitely Not if you know the procedure was not performed,

Not Completely if the procedure was performed some of the time or to some extent,

Definitely Yes if you know the procedure was performed correctly and all of the time.

After the test is completed, for all items marked *Not Sure*, find the answer from the staff member(s) who knows what was done. For all items answered *Definitely Not* or *Not Completely*, correct the situation and reread the sections of the manual dealing with those items. If many answers are in the categories of *Not Completely* or *Definitely Not*, this should be a signal that the entire

Daytime Program (Part 1) should be read again with special emphasis on those topics.

Problems will be prevented if the trainer and Supervisor fill in the answers together after each resident is trained until such time as no resident presents a problem.

Check only one answer for each question. Answer all questions.

	Not Sure	Definitely Not	Not Completely	Definitely Yes
Training				
Was the resident able to walk, see, and use 1 arm and hand?	____	____	____	____
Was a medical examination given for possible urinary or bowel problems?	____	____	____	____
Was training given in the same toilet the resident was to use later?	____	____	____	____
Was only 1 resident trained at a time until the trainer became proficient?	____	____	____	____
Were no more than 3 residents trained at any 1 time by 1 trainer?	____	____	____	____
Was the first resident trained by a new trainer the most manageable resident?	____	____	____	____
Was training conducted all day (8 hours or more) and was it uninterrupted?	____	____	____	____
Were distractions by other residents and staff in the toilet training area eliminated?	____	____	____	____
Did you use all the training materials, especially the pants alarm and urine alert?	____	____	____	____
Did the signaling apparatuses function properly?	____	____	____	____
Did you praise the resident enthusiastically and immediately when he toileted?	____	____	____	____
Did you give the praise and candy reward immediately and every time?	____	____	____	____
Did you remove outer garments during training?	____	____	____	____
Did the resident enjoy the candy or other edible rewards you used?	____	____	____	____
Did the resident drink 2 cups of fluid every half-hour?	____	____	____	____
Did the resident stop resisting your graduated guidance?	____	____	____	____

	Not Sure	Definitely Not	Not Completely	Definitely Yes

Training, cont.

Was the graduated guidance progressively reduced?

Did you completely refrain from guidance unless the resident failed to act?

Was the reminder to toilet progressively reduced to slight gestures only and with no verbal instructions?

Did you always stand next to the resident and shadow every action on each prompted toileting?

Did training at the start of a day use exactly the same level of prompting as at the end of the previous day?

Did the resident raise and lower his pants with no manual guidance and no prompting?

When outer garments were added, was the resident taught to raise and lower them?

Did you keep the record of what happened every single toileting trial?

Did you keep the resident on the toilet seat for the full 20 minutes if he did not urinate?

Did you conduct a dry-pants inspection and reward every 5 minutes?

Did you praise enthusiastically when you rewarded?

Did you always require the resident to feel his dry pants during the inspection?

When an accident occurred, did you always express immediate verbal and gestural disapproval?

Did you give Brief Cleanliness Training and Positive Practice after every accident?

During Brief Cleanliness Training and Positive Practice, did you require the resident to move rapidly?

	Not Sure	Definitely Not	Not Completely	Definitely Yes
Training, cont.				
During Positive Practice, did you speak only in a neutral tone of voice?	_____	_____	_____	_____
After an accident, did you omit the dry-pants rewards?	_____	_____	_____	_____
Did you give several Positive Practice trials after every accident?	_____	_____	_____	_____
Did you react to bowel movements in the same manner as to urinations?	_____	_____	_____	_____
Self-Initiations				
After the resident's first self-initiation, did you completely stop prompting him to the toilet?	_____	_____	_____	_____
Even after a self-initiation, did you continue to give guidance for dressing if needed?	_____	_____	_____	_____
After the first self-initiation, did you fade out the candy rewards for toileting?	_____	_____	_____	_____
After the first self-initiation, did you give the fluids after each self-initiated toileting rather than on the half-hour?	_____	_____	_____	_____
After the first self-initiation, did you fade out the drinks?	_____	_____	_____	_____
After the first self-initiation, did you move the resident's chair farther from the toilet?	_____	_____	_____	_____
After the first self-initiation, did you increase the time between dry-pants inspections?	_____	_____	_____	_____
Did you give 30 minutes of Full Cleanliness Training and Positive Practice after every accident?	_____	_____	_____	_____
Possible Problems During Training				
Did you always use graduated guidance whenever the resident refused to perform a task?	_____	_____	_____	_____
If the resident became unmanageable, did you require him to lie on his bed until he calmed down?	_____	_____	_____	_____

	Not Sure	Definitely Not	Not Completely	Definitely Yes

Possible Problems During Training, cont.

After he had calmed down, did you require the resident to complete the task that had been interrupted by his tantrum?

Did the resident toilet himself 9 times before you terminated his training?

Did you use rewards to teach hyperactive residents to sit on the toilet seat?

Did you modify the procedure for residents who had special physical problems?

If the trainee attends school, did you coordinate your training efforts with the school personnel?

Maintenance

During the Maintenance Program, were at least 6 regularly scheduled dry-pants inspections always made each day, especially prior to each meal and at bedtime?

Were several spontaneous dry-pants inspections always made each day?

Was the resident's meal, bedtime, or snack always postponed whenever he had wet prior to these occasions?

Were all of the Maintenance Supervisors enthusiastic when praising the resident for keeping his pants dry?

When the resident wet during an activity, was that activity always terminated until 30 minutes of Full Cleanliness Training and Positive Practice had been given?

Was a specific certified staff member assigned as Maintenance Supervisor on each working shift?

Did the entire ward staff take turns in serving as the Maintenance Supervisor?

Was certification as a Maintenance Supervisor always postponed until a staff member demonstrated competency in conducting all facets of the Maintenance Program?

	Not Sure	Definitely Not	Not Completely	Definitely Yes

Maintenance, cont.

Did a second certified staff member serve as an Assistant Maintenance Supervisor on each shift? _____ _____ _____ _____

Was the Maintenance Supervisor on each shift relieved of competing duties? _____ _____ _____ _____

Did you have fewer than 10 residents on the Maintenance Program at any 1 time? _____ _____ _____ _____

Was each Daily Maintenance Record sheet always filled in completely and accurately and initialed by the appropriate Maintenance Supervisor and posted conspicuously? _____ _____ _____ _____

Was the Monthly Daytime Accident Chart filled out correctly each day? _____ _____ _____ _____

Did the resident stay dry for 2 consecutive weeks before being discontinued from the Maintenance Program? _____ _____ _____ _____

On Maintenance, were the residents wearing clothing that they could raise and lower easily? _____ _____ _____ _____

After the resident had finished the Maintenance Program, was he still required to clean up and change himself after an accident? _____ _____ _____ _____

Institutional and Staff Support

Did the Ward Supervisor or someone in a position of authority take responsibility for the toilet training program? _____ _____ _____ _____

Did you obtain the active cooperation and continued support of the Institutional Director? _____ _____ _____ _____

Did you provide the Institutional Director and other supervisors with a monthly progress report of the training results? _____ _____ _____ _____

Did you discuss the training program with the entire ward staff prior to instituting the program and convince all of them of the need for the program? _____ _____ _____ _____

Did you observe each Maintenance Supervisor's actual performance during the Maintenance Program? _____ _____ _____ _____

PART 2 :: NIGHTTIME TOILET TRAINING

CHAPTER 10

A NIGHTTIME TOILET TRAINING PROCEDURE FOR ELIMINATING BED-WETTING

Bed-Wetting vs. Daytime Wetting

The previous section of this manual described procedures for eliminating daytime incontinence. Here we will consider the problem of nighttime incontinence, technically designated as enuresis or more commonly, bed-wetting. Among non-retarded normal children living at home, bed-wetting is far more common than daytime accidents. While almost all normal children stop having daytime accidents by the time they begin school at about four to five years of age, their bed-wetting often persists into adolescence. Statistics show that at the age of six, about ten percent of normal children still wet their beds. The same relationships apply to retarded persons but to a greater extent. Bed-wetting often continues for many years after daytime training has been achieved, often lasting throughout the adult years. If a retardate is having accidents during the day, he almost certainly is wetting his bed at night as well. Conversely, if a retardate is not wetting his bed at night, he almost certainly is also not having accidents during the day.

Prevalence of Bed-Wetting

For normal, non-retarded bed-wetters, a procedure has been developed for eliminating bed-wetting. This procedure uses an apparatus that sounds a loud signal as soon as the person starts to wet his bed (see p. 111). This procedure has been found to be effective for about ninety percent of bed-wetters and usually requires about three weeks of usage on the average. Unfortunately, this procedure is not effective for retardates; they require a different procedure. Bed-wetting among retardates is most evident among the profoundly and severely retarded as was also true of daytime accidents. In a typical institutional ward for the profoundly retarded, about one-half or more of the residents may not toilet themselves independently during the day. At night, however, as many as three-fourths of the residents may wet their beds regularly. The higher the level of functioning of the retarded, the lower is the frequency of bed-wetting but even among the higher levels of retardation, bed-wetting is common if they are institutionalized.

Why Bed-Wetting Is a Problem

The same factors that cause daytime accidents in the institutionalized profoundly retarded also contribute to the persistence of bed-wetting at night and have been discussed in Chapter 2. In summary, these factors are lower learning capacity, physical and sensory disabilities, relative insensitivity to staff disapproval, and failure of staff to provide disapproval. In addition, bed-wetting is probably more frequent than daytime wetting since the individual is less alert and attentive when asleep than when awake, detection of an accident is delayed until morning, and the inconvenience of interrupting one's sleep to toilet oneself is greater than the mild inconvenience of walking to the toilet when awake.

Train Daytime Continence First

Since daytime continence is easier to learn than nighttime continence, training to eliminate bed-wetting should not be attempted until the bed-wetter has first learned to toilet himself independently during the day. If the bed-wetter has accidents during the day when he is mentally alert and attentive to his state, when his wetting is easily and quickly detected, and when toileting is not interfering with his sleep, then efforts to train him at night will be premature when all of these additional difficulties are present. Do not attempt to eliminate bed-wetting if the individual is still wetting during the day. First train him to be dry during the day; then train him to be dry at night.

Training Strategy

If the retarded bed-wetter has learned to toilet himself during the day, we can assume that he has several skills that need not be taught. He has learned to be sensitive to his bladder pressure signals; he knows how to inhibit urination; he can raise and lower his pants; he knows where the toilet is and how to use it; he does not wait for someone to prompt him; and he has learned that wetting brings disapproval. He is unable, however, to generalize these habits to the nighttime situation when he is less alert and preoccupied with sleep. To assist the retardate in transferring his habits to the sleeping situation, the following procedures are used.

Increased Fluid Intake

As in the daytime training, he is given large quantities of fluid at regular and frequent intervals during the night. The frequent urinations that result can be given immediate trainer approval when done in the toilet or immediate trainer disapproval when bed-wetting results.

Immediate Detection of Accidents

An apparatus is used to immediately signal the trainer when bed-wetting starts. This immediacy of detection of nighttime accidents facilitates learning. The apparatus is the same one noted previously for use with non-retarded bed-wetters.

Disapproval and Nighttime Cleanliness Training

Disapproval is given immediately upon detection of bed-wetting as signaled by the bed-wetting apparatus (wet-bed alarm). The trainer reprimands the bed-wetter and requires him to clean the bed by removing the soiled linen and remaking the bed with fresh linen. The verbal reprimand and the required cleaning of the bed teaches the bed-wetter that bed-wetting is discouraged as much as is wet pants during the day.

Rewards for Correct Toileting

Approval and rewards are given for correct toileting. After the individual has walked to the toilet, he is given praise and tasty foods as soon as he has urinated in the toilet bowl. This reward reminds the bed-wetter that the trainer is as pleased with him for eliminating in the toilet at night as he is for his correct toileting during the day.

Positive Practice of Correct Toileting

Positive Practice in traveling between the bed and the toilet is given whenever an accident occurs. The darkness and unfamiliar appearance of the bedroom at night can cause apprehension and direction difficulties. By requiring the bed-wetter to practice several trips from his bed to the toilet whenever he wets his bed, he is given practice and proficiency as well as the realization that this act is important and required.

Self-Initiation Training

The bed-wetter is taught to initiate the trip to the toilet from his bed by having the trainer diminish the degree of guidance and instructions used in awakening the bed-wetter. The trainer decreases his prompts from manual guidance to a mere touch to a slight gesture and decreases his verbal instructions to a mere whisper.

Who Can Be Trained?

A retardate who has learned to toilet himself during the day can generally be trained very quickly to keep his bed dry at night. Exceptions to this rule are the very young or the very old, both for reasons of their inability to walk easily and limitations on their bladder control. A young retarded child, two to four years old, may be able to interrupt his play activities to walk to the toilet during the day, but be discouraged from climbing down from an elevated crib at night. Similarly, the elderly retarded who walk with difficulty during the day will be understandably apprehensive about falling while walking in a darkened hallway at night. The physical condition of the bladder is more important at night since nighttime continence depends more on the ability to inhibit urination. For the very young child, below four years of age, the bladder and sphincter muscles may not be sufficiently developed to allow the retention of urine throughout an entire night. Similarly, the loss of elasticity of the bladder muscles in the elderly often prevents the nightlong retention of urine. When these problems of retention capacity are only marginal, the bed-wetting problem is solved by motivating the bed-wetter to interrupt his sleep once or twice during the night to toilet himself. With severe retention limitations he would be required to interrupt his sleep continuously. Understandably, the severely bladder-impaired geriatric retardate will present a major problem and failures for them should be anticipated occasionally and sympathetically tolerated. For the young retarded child, time should be allowed for the bladder to develop if problems are encountered.

How Long Does Training Require?

The average bed-wetter can be trained in only one or two nights starting at bedtime and continuing until the normal time for rising in the morning. After this intensive training, the average bed-wetter will wet his bed about once or twice during the next two weeks and about once during the following month. Thereafter, bed-wetting is likely to occur only under such understandable circumstances as a cold room temperature that discourages self-toileting, excessive fluid intake prior to bedtime, illness, or intestinal disorders. Only rarely does training require two nights, and almost never does it require three nights.

Detection and Reward of Correct Toileting

The urine alert apparatus (see p. 29) is inserted in the toilet bowl so that an immediate signal will be given to the trainer at the instant urination begins. The trainer then shows his approval by praising and hugging the individual, smiling, and giving him the tasty edible rewards. Only the verbal praise should be given at the start of urination so that urination can be completed. The automatic signal provided by the urine alert is useful for a second reason. If the bed-wetter awakens himself to urinate in the toilet stool while the trainer is occupied elsewhere, the trainer can still reward him by proceeding to the toilet when he hears the signal.

Detection of Bed-Wetting

The major causes of bed-wetting are that the individual is not sufficiently alert to realize that he is urinating and that other persons do not observe the act of wetting as readily as during the day. The wet-bed alarm devices overcome these problems by producing a sound as soon as bed-wetting starts, thereby alerting the bed-wetter and others. Several commercial models of these bed-wetter alarms are available.[†] A flat pad or pair of pads is placed under the bed sheet. When urine moistens the pad, a signal sounds and continues to sound until the trainer terminates it by a switch on the apparatus. The loudness of the signal is adjustable on some of the more expensive apparatuses; if so, the loudness should be adjusted so as to be easily heard by the trainer. If the loudness is not adjustable, the trainer should remain in those locations where he can hear the signal, or transfer the bed to an area where the signal can be heard.

Training Sequence

Have the necessary materials shown in Table 17 present before beginning. Place the urine alert in the toilet stool. Place the wet-bed alarm on the mattress before bedtime. Have a variety of fluids available, such as water, soda, juices, and punches, selecting those that are favored by the bed-wetter. Favored candies and tasty edibles such as sugar-coated cereals, M&M candies, and chocolates are needed. These candies may be carried conveniently in an apron so that they are always available. A kitchen timer or pocket timer (see p. 28) is used to provide an audible signal every hour. The timer is reset each time it has timed out. Attach the Nighttime Toilet Training Checklist (see Figure 12, p. 116) to a clipboard. The clipboard, fluids, and cups may all be placed on a cart so that they can be conveniently brought to the bedside. Ensure that the bed-wetter has an opportunity to toilet himself before bedtime but do not prompt him to do so lest he become dependent on the prompts. Require him to drink about 2 cups of fluid just before bedtime.

As outlined in Figure 11, every hour on the hour mark, awaken the bed-wetter and require him to feel his dry bed. Reward him with an edible and praise for not wetting his bed. He should then be required to proceed to the toilet area and to be seated on the stool which contains the urine alert. Require him to be seated

---

† For ordering information, see p. 135.

on the stool for 5 minutes. If he does not urinate within 5 minutes, direct him back to his room where he is given 2 cups of fluid before returning to his bed. If he urinates before the 5 minutes have

---

Table 17   Materials Required for Nighttime Training

---

1. Drinking glasses or cups
2. Urine alerts (p. 29)
3. Variety of fluids (p. 34)
4. Candies and edibles (p. 33)
5. Kitchen timer or pocket timer
6. Cart
7. Wet-bed alarm
8. Nighttime Toilet Training Checklist (Figure 12, p. 116)
9. Clipboard

Figure 11   Flow Chart of the Nighttime Training Sequence

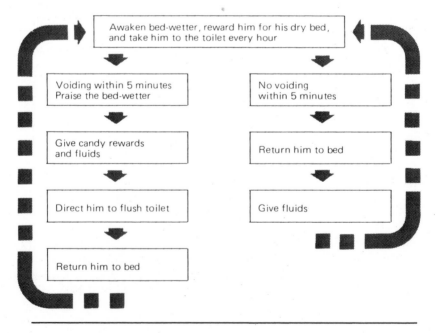

elapsed, immediately praise him. After urination is completed, embrace him, stroke his shoulders, give him the candy rewards, and also 2 cups of fluids. Direct him to flush the toilet. He is then directed to his room where he returns to his bed. This regular toileting procedure is repeated every hour as signaled by the timer.

Self-Initiation

If the bed-wetter independently toilets himself during the night, the trainer should reward him as described above. During a self-initiated toileting, the trainer should remain as inconspicuous as possible, limiting his interactions to providing rewards and assistance should the bed-wetter become disoriented on his way back to bed. The urine alert which was placed in the toilet bowl will have signaled the trainer that urination occurred. The urine alert apparatus is cleaned out and reset after each use.

Accidents

Nighttime Cleanliness Training and Disapproval

The purpose of Nighttime Cleanliness Training is to teach the bed-wetter that he is responsible for cleaning the bed that he has wet. Table 18 shows the steps required. The bed-wetter is awakened if he has not already been awakened by the alarm. The trainer then shows his disapproval by telling him that he must not wet his bed. Since the bed-wetter is not likely to be quite alert and attentive, the trainer should have him sit up in bed and gain eye contact while

---

Table 18   Nighttime Cleanliness Training and Disapproval for Bed-Wetting*
(Accident signaled by the wet-bed alarm)

1. Awaken the bed-wetter by grasping his shoulders.
2. Tell the bed-wetter, "No, you wet your bed" and show displeasure on your face.
3. Turn off the wet-bed alarm and send bed-wetter to the toilet.
4. Remove wet-bed alarm from the bed and wipe it dry.
5. *Cleanliness Training:* Require the bed-wetter to:
   a. remove his soiled linen
   b. carry the soiled linen to the appropriate receptacle
   c. obtain clean linen
   d. remake his bed after you reconnect the wet-bed alarm and put on the bottom sheet

---

the trainer expresses his disapproval. If necessary, grasp his shoulders to maintain the raised position and to orient him such that he is making close face-to-face contact. The trainer then sends him to the toilet. While the bed-wetter is gone, the trainer removes the wet-bed alarm apparatus since the bed-wetter should not be allowed to handle the apparatus. When the bed-wetter returns to the dormitory, the trainer requires him to remove the soiled linen, wipe the mattress if necessary, place the soiled linen in whatever container is normally used for that purpose, obtain fresh linen from the usual source, and carry the linen to the bed. The trainer then cleans and reconnects the wet-bed alarm apparatus and covers it with the bottom sheet himself to avoid having the bed-wetter handle it. The bed-wetter completes the making of the bed by adding a new top sheet and blanket. The trainer speaks to him only in a neutral non-critical tone and uses gentle manual guidance when necessary (see Graduated Guidance, p. 37).

Positive Practice

After the bed-wetter has remade his bed, using the Nighttime Cleanliness Training procedure, he is given about 10 practice trials in going to the toilet. The steps in this Positive Practice are outlined in Table 19. The trainer returns the bed-wetter to the bed and allows him to lie down for about 2 minutes. At the end of the 2 minutes, the trainer requires the bed-wetter to arise from the bed and

---

Table 19   Positive Practice for Bed-Wetting*
(Given immediately following Nighttime Cleanliness Training)

---

1. Require bed-wetter to lie down on his bed for about 2 minutes.

2. At the end of the 2 minutes, rouse the bed-wetter and escort him to the toilet.

3. Require the bed-wetter to lower his pants and sit on toilet for about 30 seconds.

4. At the end of the 30 seconds, escort him back to his bed.

Repeat the above steps about 10 times or until 45 minutes have elapsed since the wet-bed alarm sounded. Do not reward or praise during this required practice. Use verbal instructions and graduated guidance, if necessary, fading them out on each succeeding trial.

---

walk to the toilet. The bed-wetter is then required to lower his pants and sit on the toilet for about 30 seconds. After 30 seconds, the bed-wetter is directed to raise his pants and proceed back to his bed. The above steps are repeated 10 times or until 45 minutes have elapsed since the wet-bed alarm sounded. The bed-wetter is required to relax on his bed for 2 minutes in order to simulate the normal sleeping situation in which he is expected to rouse himself from a relaxed state. Graduated guidance is given whenever the bed-wetter fails to initiate a requested movement. The guidance should be faded out rapidly, and the trainer should be located behind the bed-wetter in order to approximate the desired normal situation in which the individual toilets himself when no one is present. If the bed-wetter voids in the toilet during a Positive Practice trial, he should not be rewarded; this behavior should be ignored. Otherwise, he may deliberately wet his bed in order to obtain the reward.

Recording During Training

Nighttime Toilet Training Checklist

Keeping records during training permits the objective assessment of the bed-wetter's progress. For example, the trainer relies completely on the records to determine when the bed-wetter has completed training (see p. 116). Figure 12 shows the Nighttime Toilet Training Checklist that is used during the training as a step-by-step guide and to record training results. Each night of training will require a new page for each bed-wetter. The Training Checklist is divided into hour intervals. Five entries are made each hour. The trainer marks a check beside Step 1 after the bed-wetter has been awakened and directed to the toilet; Step 2 is for correct eliminations during the prompted toiletings; Step 3 is checked if the bed-wetter did not eliminate during the 5 minutes he sat on the toilet; Step 4 is for recording the exact times of correct toiletings that were self-initiated; and Step 5 is for recording exact times at which any accidents occurred. The nightly training results are summarized at the bottom of Figure 12. Under "Total Toileting Opportunities," enter the number of hourly prompted toiletings and self-initiations (Step 1 row plus Step 4 row). "Total Appropriate Urinations" refers to the number of times the bed-wetter urinated at the hourly toiletings plus the number of self-initiations that may have occurred (Step 2 row plus Step 4 row). The "Percent of Appropriate Urinations" is calculated by dividing the number of Total Toileting Opportunities into the number of Total Appropriate Urinations and multiplying by 100. "Total Accidents" refers to the number of times the bed-wetter wet his bed (the Step 5 row total).

When Is Training Complete?

The purpose of nighttime toilet training is to teach the bed-wetter to inhibit wetting his bed and to toilet himself independently should

---

Figure 12   Nighttime Toilet Training Checklist*

Resident's Name __Sam T.__   Date __4/ 11 / 73__
(See p. 111)
Check each item when completed.

Part 1   Check the following before beginning training.

✓ 1.   Was the bed-wetter given access to the toilet prior to his retiring for the night?
✓ 2.   Was the bed-wetter given fluids prior to his retiring for the night?
✓ 3.   Has the wet-bed alarm been placed and made operable?

Part 2   Are the materials listed below available?

✓ 1.   Urine alert in the toilet bowl
✓ 2.   Drinking glass or cup
✓ 3.   Assortment of fluids
✓ 4.   Edible treats
✓ 5.   Nighttime Toilet Training Checklist
✓ 6.   Clean linen (sheets and blankets)

Part 3   Nighttime Toilet Training Sequence
           (Start exactly on the hour, repeating the following steps every hour.)

	P.M.						A.M.						
	7	8	9	10	11	12	1	2	3	4	5	6	7
1. Awakened bed-wetter using the minimal possible prompt and directed him to sit on toilet.	✓	✓	✓	✓	✓	✓	✓	✓	✓	✓	✓	✓	✓
2. When bed-wetter voided within 5 minutes, gave edibles, praise, and fluids while seated, directed him to flush toilet, and directed him back to bed.	✓	✓	✓		✓	✓		✓		✓	✓		✓
3. If bed-wetter did not void within 5 minutes, gave no reward, directed him back to his bed where he was given 2 cups of fluid.				✓			✓		✓			✓	
4. Self-Initiated Toileting—Gave edibles and praise, but not fluids. Note exact time.								1:22				6:3	
5. Accidents—Gave Nighttime Cleanliness Training and Positive Practice. Note exact time.				10:10									

Total Toileting Opportunities _____15_____   Total Appropriate Urinations ___11___

Percent of Appropriate Urinations ___73%___   Total Accidents____I____

Comments:

---

he be unable to inhibit urination throughout an entire night. Thus, the retarded person can be considered continent at night if he does not wet his bed. Whether he attains continence by inhibition or by arising at night to use the toilet is not critical, since normal individuals remain continent by either method. The training program has been designed to teach the bed-wetter both of these methods of maintaining continence. As a result, the bed-wetter is considered trained when he meets both of the following conditions: (1) he

116

must not wet his bed more than once during the training night and (2) he must urinate in the toilet during at least 50 percent of all his toileting opportunities. For example, if there were 10 prompted hourly toiletings during the night, the bed-wetter must urinate in the toilet at least 5 of those 10 times. Any self-initiations would also be counted as in computing the percent of appropriate urinations. As mentioned previously, most bed-wetters will reach the training criteria within one night and will almost never require more than three nights.

Maintenance

The former bed-wetter has been trained not to wet his bed. He has demonstrated that he knows where to urinate at night should the need arise, and that his bed-wetting will no longer be tolerated. We must now ensure that he will continue to refrain from wetting his bed.

Several factors motivate normal persons to remain continent at night: the unpleasantness of sleeping in a soiled bed, being awakened by an accident, and the time and effort required the following morning to change the stained linen. These factors do not operate for many retarded individuals, however, since they have grown accustomed to sleeping in a wet bed, and they are not held responsible for correcting their accidents because of their obvious reduced learning capacity.

The Maintenance Program has been designed to motivate the newly trained individual by requiring him to assume responsibility for his actions. This responsibility consists of requiring the individual to engage in Nighttime Cleanliness Training and Positive Practice whenever an accident occurs as signaled by the wet-bed alarm. The Nighttime Cleanliness Training and Positive Practice are the same procedures used during training. Additionally, the trainer rewards the individual's newly demonstrated independence each morning by praising him for not wetting his bed. These motivators are gradually faded out as the individual demonstrates his desire not to wet his bed. The wet-bed alarm is removed. Any future accidents are then corrected by the retarded individual changing his linen in the morning in the same manner as non-retarded persons.

Overview of the Maintenance Program

The Maintenance Program consists of two phases. The first phase is the Monitored Maintenance phase and is begun on the night immediately following training. During this phase, the wet-bed alarm continues to be attached to the former bed-wetter's bed. Monitored

117

Maintenance differs from training in that (1) the former bed-wetter is not awakened during the night unless an accident is signaled and (2) no fluids are given. The Monitored Maintenance phase is terminated when the individual does not wet his bed for 7 consecutive nights. The second phase, designated simply as Maintenance, involves removing the wet-bed alarm and only checking the individual's bedding in the morning. This phase should be considered as the normal reaction to accidents (see p. 119). If the former bed-wetter has 2 accidents during a 7-day period, he is placed back on the Monitored Maintenance phase until he does not wet his bed for 7 consecutive nights.

When the Former Bed-Wetter is Found Wet

When an accident is signaled during the Monitored Maintenance phase, the same Nighttime Cleanliness Training and Positive Practice procedures described during training should be given (see p. 113). During the Maintenance phase, when the individual's bedding is discovered wet or stained the next morning, he should be given Cleanliness Training. If the trainer is preoccupied at that time, the Cleanliness Training may be abbreviated or delayed until supervision is possible. In every case, the bed-wetter should not dress or proceed to breakfast until he has completed remaking his bed so that he will learn that when he wets his bed, he will be held responsible for remaking it. Unavoidable accidents caused by infection or virus should be dealt with sympathetically and the bed-wetter not held responsible for them.

Continued Accidents During Maintenance

If, after 4 weeks of Maintenance, the bed-wetter is continuing to have 2 or more accidents per week, corrective action must be taken. The nature of this action will depend on the source of the individual's continued bed-wetting. Generally, the problem will stem from one of three sources. First, the bed-wetter may not have been completely trained to be dry during the day. The daytime toilet habits should be evaluated and daytime toilet training given if necessary. If daytime training is needed, discontinue the nighttime program until the individual has successfully completed the daytime Maintenance Program. A second, common explanation is that the Nighttime Cleanliness Training and Positive Practice are not being conducted properly. To solve this problem, see "Continued Accidents During Maintenance," p. 82. The third explanation is that the bed-wetter may have physical problems which prevent him from controlling his bladder or which interfere with his walking to the toilet. The solutions to this last problem have been discussed in previous sections (see Medical Examination, p. 25, and Physically Handicapped, p. 68).

Normal Reaction to Accidents

Following the Monitored Maintenance, standard practice should be to inspect the individual's bedding for stains or wetting every morning. If his bed is stained or wet, he should be required to remake it (Nighttime Cleanliness Training). Also, remind the bed-wetter that should his accidents continue, he will be required to practice going to the toilet (Positive Practice) and that his bed-wetting will have to be more closely monitored (wet-bed alarm).

CHAPTER 11

INSTITUTIONAL FACTORS IN NIGHTTIME TOILET TRAINING

When bed-wetting occurs in a large institution, training is complicated by factors that do not exist in a family setting or in a small institution. The large number of residents and staff creates the same problems noted in Part 1 of determining who is a bed-wetter, who should be the trainer, supervision of the attendants, record keeping, and communication among staff members. Since many of the suggested procedures are similar to those described in Part 1, this chapter will present a briefer treatment of institutional factors.

Selection of Trainers

If the institutional ward has adopted the daytime toileting program described in Part 1, it is suggested that the daytime trainer also serve as the nighttime trainer. Of course, if many residents are bed-wetters, a different staff member may be needed to be on duty regularly at night in which case he could be trained in his duties by the daytime trainer. The daytime trainer ensures the new nighttime trainer's proficiency by demonstrating to him the Nighttime Cleanliness Training (p. 113) and Positive Practice procedures (p. 114), how to reward properly, and the appropriate way to express displeasure for accidents.

Recording Prior to Training

In order to determine the extent of the ward's bed-wetting problem you may wish to obtain a pre-training record. Figure 13 illustrates the Pre-Training Bed-Wetting Record that can be used in making this assessment. The trainer should check the bedding of suspected bed-wetters each morning for 7 days. If the bedding is wet or stained, a W (Wet) is recorded in the appropriate space. Similarly, if the bedding is not wet, a D (Dry) is recorded beside the resident's name. If this record is maintained for one week as shown in Figure 13, almost all chronic bed-wetters will be identified, including those who wet only occasionally.

Dormitory Arrangements

Since the bed-wetting alarm sounds a loud signal, other residents may be awakened. Generally, the other residents will become accustomed to this sound after their initial curiosity just as they have become accustomed to the loud sound of nearby trains or air con-

---

Figure 13 Pre-Training Bed-Wetting Record*

W = Wet   Ward __1__
D = Dry   Date __3/ 15/ 73__

Resident's Name	1	2	Night 3	4	5	6	7	Total Wets
JIMMY T.	W	W	W	W	W	W	D	6
BILLY G.	W	W	W	W	D	W	W	6
EddiE P.	W	W	W	W	W	W	W	7
DAVid K.	W	D	D	W	W	W	W	5
SAM T.	D	D	D	W	W	D	W	3
John B.	W	W	W	W	W	W	D	6
GEorgE A.	W	W	D	W	W	W	W	6
BrucE Y.	W	W	W	W	W	W	W	7
CaRL D.	D	W	D	D	W	W	D	3
RonniE G.	W	W	W	W	W	D	W	6

ditioners. Their initial distraction can be reduced by locating all residents with alarms on their beds in the same room, or reserving a special area for the resident who is to be trained that evening. The signal will sound for only a few seconds if the staff members are prompt in reacting to the signal.

Maintenance Supervisor

Certification of Proficiency and Duties

As was the case during the daytime Maintenance Program, the entire ward staff should become involved in the nighttime Maintenance Program. On each shift, a staff member will be designated to serve as Maintenance Supervisor for that shift. The staff members are trained by the toilet trainer, then certified (see Certification of Proficiency, p. 75). The evening and night shift Maintenance Supervisors provide Nighttime Cleanliness Training and Positive Practice Training when accidents are signaled by the wet-bed alarm during the Monitored Maintenance phase. The day shift Maintenance Supervisor inspects the beds and arranges for the residents to clean up their accidents from the previous night. The scheduling of Maintenance Supervisors has been described elsewhere (see Scheduling, p. 77). The Maintenance duties of the evening and night shift Supervisors should not conflict with other duties since few regularly scheduled duties exist at night. Also, bed-wetting during the Monitored Maintenance phase should average fewer than two accidents per resident per week; therefore, a staff member will spend only a minor portion of his time conducting the Nighttime Cleanliness Training and Positive Practice procedures.

Number of Residents
in the Maintenance Program

No serious limitation exists on the number of residents who may be in the Maintenance Program at one time. Theoretically, a problem will occur if several residents wet their beds at about the same time. This is extremely rare, however, since very few accidents are occurring. Of course, if two staff members are on duty, the second staff member can react to a second bed-wetter and the rare simultaneous wettings will not be a problem.

Recording

The Nightly Maintenance Record

The form for recording nighttime accidents is similar to the Daily Maintenance Record. A sample Nightly Maintenance Record sheet is shown in Figure 14. This record is used: (1) to show which staff members on each shift have been assigned as Maintenance Supervisors, (2) to ensure that the wet-bed alarms are placed on the beds of residents in the Monitored Maintenance phase, and (3) to provide a record of the accidents including the time the resident was discovered wet, the disposition of the accident, and the initials of the Maintenance Supervisor who handled the accidents.

Prior to the residents' bedtime, the Maintenance Supervisor lists the names of residents who are in both phases of the Maintenance Program (see p. 117). A check mark in the column designated, *Requires Wet-Bed Alarm*, should be made beside the name of each resident in the Monitored Maintenance phase. The early evening Maintenance Supervisor then places a wet-bed alarm on these residents' beds. After all the alarms have been placed, the

---

Figure 14 Nightly Maintenance Record*

Ward __1__

Date __4/12/73__

Supervisor's initials when wet-bed alarms are placed __S.T.__

Afternoon Maintenance Supervisor __Sandy Thomas__
Afternoon Asst. Maintenance Supervisor __Clara Beck__
Night Maintenance Supervisor __Carl Stephens__
Night Asst. Maintenance Supervisor __Randy Klien__
Morning Maintenance Supervisor __Susan Kopeck__
Morning Asst. Maintenance Supervisor __Edna Ripley__

Nightly Accident Chart

(If an accident is unavoidable, place an asterisk beside the resident's name.)

Resident's name	Requires wet-bed alarm	Time found wet (Cleanliness Training and Positive Practice given)	Supervisor's initials when completed
JIMMY T.	✓		
John B.	✓	11:37 / 3:42	C.S / C.S
Bruce Y.	✓	2:13	C.S
Carl D.	✓		
Billy G.			
David K.			
Sam T.	✓	4:22	C.S
George A.		6:30	R.K.
Ronnie G. *		6:30 (sick)	J.K.
		No Cleanliness Training or positive practice given	

Supervisor initials the space provided at the upper portion of the form. The Supervisors also initial the last column after they have recorded a resident's accident and that Nighttime Cleanliness Training and Positive Practice were given.

Monthly Nighttime Accident Chart

The Monthly Nighttime Accident Chart shown in Figure 15 is similar in design and function to the monthly form used to record daytime continence. The night shift Supervisor records the results of the previous night from the Nightly Maintenance Record. The Monthly Nighttime Accident Chart provides the following information:

1. When to terminate the Monitored Maintenance phase (see Overview of the Maintenance Program, p. 117). The Monitored Maintenance phase is terminated when a resident remains dry for 7 consecutive nights. This information can be gathered easily by circling the first 7 blocks beginning with the date the resident enters Monitored Maintenance. If no accidents are recorded in any of these blocks, the wet-bed alarm is removed and the resident's bed is checked only in the morning. When an accident is recorded in one of the circled dates, the Supervisor should circle the subsequent 7 nights. Continue to circle 7 nights from

---

Figure 15   Monthly Nighttime Accident Chart*

Instructions: Month of **APRIL 1973**
1. Fill in the names of all the ward residents at the beginning of the month.
2. Under the appropriate night, put a check mark if a resident had an accident. If none were detected, record a zero.
3. Place a capital *T* on the nights the resident receives training.
4. Circle the first 7 nights beginning with the date the resident enters the Monitored Maintenance phase. If an accident is recorded in one of these circles, circle 7 subsequent nights.
5. Do not record accidents that are marked with an asterisk as unavoidable on the Nightly Maintenance Record.

Night

Resident's Name	1	2	3	4	5	6	7	8	9	10	11	12	13	14	15	16	17	18	19	20	21	22	23	24	25	26	27	28	29	30	31	Total nights wet for the month
JIMMY T.	✓	✓	✓	✓	T	ⓞ	ⓞ	ⓞ	ⓞ	ⓞ	ⓞ	ⓞ	ⓞ	o	o	o	o	o	o	o	o	o	o	o	o	o	o	o	o	o		4
BILLY G.	✓	✓	T	T	ⓞ	ⓞ	ⓞ	ⓞ	ⓞ	ⓞ	o	o	o	o	o	✓	o	o	o	o	o	✓	o	o	o	o	o	o	o	o		4
EDDIE P(m)	ⓞ	ⓞ	ⓞ	o	o	o	o	o	o	o	✓	o	o	o	o	o	o	o	o	✓	o	o	o	o	o	o	o	o	o	✓		3
DAVID K.	o	o	o	o	o	o	o	o	o	o	o	o	o	o	o	o	o	o	o	o	o	o	o	o	o	o	o	o	o	o		0
SAM T.	✓	✓	✓	o	✓	o	o	o	✓	✓	T	ⓞ	ⓞ	ⓞ	ⓞ	ⓞ	ⓞ	ⓞ	ⓞ	ⓞ	ⓞ	ⓞ	o	o	o	o	o	o	o	o		7
JOHN B.	✓	✓	✓	✓	✓	✓	T	ⓞ	ⓞ	ⓞ	ⓞ	ⓞ	ⓞ	ⓞ	ⓞ	ⓞ	o	o	o	✓	o	o	o	o	o	o	o	o	o	o		9
GEORGE A.	o	o	o	o	o	o	o	o	o	o	o	o	o	o	o	o	o	o	o	o	o	o	o	o	o	o	o	o	o	o		0
BRUCE Y.	✓	✓	✓	✓	✓	T	ⓞ	ⓞ	ⓞ	ⓞ	ⓞ	ⓞ	ⓞ	ⓞ	ⓞ	ⓞ	o	o	o	o	o	✓	o	o	o	o	o	o	o	o		8
CARL D.	o	✓	✓	o	✓	T	ⓞ	ⓞ	ⓞ	ⓞ	ⓞ	ⓞ	o	o	o	o	✓	o	o	o	o	o	o	o	o	o	o	o	o	o		4
RONNIE G.	T	ⓞ	ⓞ	ⓞ	ⓞ	ⓞ	ⓞ	ⓞ	o	o	o	✓	ⓞ	ⓞ	ⓞ	ⓞ	ⓞ	ⓞ	ⓞ	ⓞ	o	o	o	o	o	o	o	o	o	o		2

Residents transferred to ward since 1st of month	1	2	3	4	5	6	7	8	9	10	11	12	13	14	15	16	17	18	19	20	21	22	23	24	25	26	27	28	29	30	31	Total nights wet for the month
ART M.																		✓	✓	✓	✓	✓	✓	✓	T	T	ⓞ	ⓞ	ⓞ			5
MACK W.																					✓	✓	✓	✓	✓	o	T	ⓞ	ⓞ			5

125

the last accident until the resident has remained dry for 7 consecutive nights.

2. The extent of bed-wetting on the ward. The form is used to complete a monthly progress report to be circulated among concerned hospital administrators (see Figure 16).

3. Residents who are continuing to wet their beds can be quickly identified so that corrective actions can be taken.

Problems

Most problems that will be encountered during the Training and Maintenance Programs have already been discussed in earlier chapters. Reference to these chapters should be made when particular problems arise. However, there are some problems which are unique to the nighttime program. These problems and their solutions are discussed below.

Urinating on the Floor

Prior to being trained, some residents have learned to urinate on the floor beside their beds or in the hallways in order to to avoid soiling their beds. These residents often attempt to continue this behavior after their training is completed. To eliminate this problem, the Maintenance Supervisor should identify which resident has the problem and should periodically check that resident and the floor area (at least twice per hour). If the resident is discovered urinating on the floor or if the Supervisor finds a puddle beside the resident's bed, he is given Full Cleanliness Training and Positive Practice as soon as the puddle is noted. The Cleanliness Training for this floor-wetting should consist of requiring the resident to clean up the puddle (see p. 55).

Roaming at Night

It is not unusual for some residents to roam about the ward during the night. If these "roamers" are bed-wetters, their roaming should be discouraged, at least until they are capable of remaining in their beds without wetting. Otherwise, detection of wetting will be difficult and delayed. When the resident is observed out of his bed, the ward staff should wait a few moments to determine if he is on his way to the toilet. When it is apparent that the resident has no desire to toilet himself, escort him to bed. Remind the resident that he should be leaving his bed only if he has to use the toilet. Once the resident has remained in bed for about one week, and without wetting, the staff may allow him to roam about at night as long as no evidence exists of renewed floor-wetting.

Ensuring Administrative Support

The nighttime toilet training program requires the same support of the Institutional Director that has been described for the daytime program. The rationale for this required support, the problems associated with institutional incontinence, and the commitments that the Institutional Director must make in order to ensure a successful program have been discussed previously in Chapter 7. These considerations are also listed in Tables 15 and 16 (pp. 90 and 91).

A Coordinator should be designated as responsible for the nighttime program. This nighttime Toilet Training Coordinator may be the daytime Coordinator or a night shift Supervisor. The important consideration is that the Coordinator provides on-the-spot supervision during the night. The duties of the Toilet Training Coordinator have been discussed previously and are listed in Table 14 (p. 89).

Figure 16   Monthly Nighttime Toilet Training Summary*

Ward _____ **1** _____
Monthly report of __**APRIL**____

	This month	Last month	Percent change
Percent of residents continent	**20**	**0**	**+20**
Percent of residents infrequently incontinent[1]	**60**	**0**	**+60**
Percent of residents regularly incontinent[2]	**20**	**100**	**−80**

Toilet Training Coordinator's signature _Edward Simpson_

Comments: _The program has been a smashing success. We are now training one resident per night. It looks as if the ward's weekly laundry load will be cut by 400%._

Institutional Director's signature _____ _James Cox_ _____

Comments: _The changes noted above are certainly impressive. I intend to direct other wards in the hospital to begin using the program._

Routing: Institutional Director and return

[1] Residents averaging less than two accidents per week

[2] Residents averaging two or more accidents per week

It will be recalled that one of the Coordinator's important functions is to keep the Institutional Director well informed on the progress of the training program by providing him with monthly progress reports. Figure 16 illustrates the Monthly Nighttime Toilet Training Summary used for this purpose. It is filled out by using information from the Monthly Nighttime Accident Chart (see Figure 15, p. 125). In calculating the various entries on the monthly summary sheet, follow the directions described on p. 89. The Institutional Director should reroute the monthly summary back to the ward so that it can be displayed as a continuous reminder of the Institutional Director's concern that nighttime incontinence be eliminated.

Chapter 12

PROBLEM IDENTIFICATION:
A SELF-TEST FOR NIGHTTIME TRAINING

Chapter 9 presented a self-test for identifying problems that might arise in daytime training. This chapter presents a self-test covering the principal procedures of the nighttime training program. Only those procedures are listed that are known to cause serious problems if omitted or conducted improperly.

The function of the following self-test is almost identical to that of the daytime training self-test. It will serve as a summary review, reminding the trainer of the critical procedures in the training program. The test answers will (1) suggest what to do if problems arise in the program by calling attention to omitted procedural details and (2) serve as a reminder of what sections of the manual should be read again. When a problem arises in the program, the trainer (and Supervisor if training is being conducted within an institution) should use this self-test as a method of discovering what procedural deviations caused the problem.

In addition, this self-test can be used before starting to train a bed-wetter as a means of becoming alert to the most critical procedures. Then the questions should be answered a second time after the first night of training, then again after the bed-wetter has completed a few days in the Maintenance Program. This anticipation of problems will help prevent them.

In answering each question, mark:

Not Sure if you are not certain of what was actually done,

Definitely Not if you know the procedure was not performed,

Not Completely if the procedure was performed some of the time or to some extent,

Definitely Yes if you know the procedure was performed correctly and all of the time.

After the test is completed, for all items marked *Not Sure*, find the answer from someone who knows what was done. For all items answered *Definitely Not* or *Not Completely,* correct the situation and reread the sections of the manual dealing with those items. If many answers are in the categories of *Not Completely* or *Definitely Not,* this should be a signal that the entire Nighttime Program (Part 2) should be read again with special emphasis on those topics.

In institutional settings, problems will be prevented if the trainer and Supervisor fill in the answers together after each resident is trained until such time as no resident presents a problem.

Check only one answer for each question. Answer all questions.

	Not Sure	Definitely Not	Not Completely	Definitely Yes
Training				
Was the bed-wetter at least 4 years of age and completely dry during the day?				
Was the first resident trained by a new trainer the most manageable resident?				
Did you use all the training materials, especially the wet-bed alarm and urine alert?				
Did the signaling apparatus function properly?				
Did the trainee enjoy the candy or other edible rewards that you used?				
Did you awaken and toilet the bed-wetter every hour?				
When you awakened him, did you require him to feel his dry bed and then praise and reward him?				
Did the bed-wetter drink at least 2 cups of fluid every hour?				
Were you enthusiastic when praising?				
Did you always provide graduated guidance when the bed-wetter did not follow instructions quickly?				
Did the bed-wetter stop resisting your graduated guidance?				
Was the graduated guidance progressively reduced?				
Did you completely refrain from guidance unless the bed-wetter failed to act?				

	Not Sure	Definitely Not	Not Completely	Definitely Yes

Training, cont.

Did you keep a record of what happened every single toileting trial?

Did you praise enthusiastically when you rewarded?

After an accident, did you awaken the bed-wetter immediately and fully, express visible disapproval, and require a full 45 minutes of Cleanliness Training and Positive Practice?

During Positive Practice, did you speak only in a neutral tone of voice?

During Positive Practice, did you always allow the bed-wetter to lie down for 2 minutes before beginning another trial?

Did you modify the procedure for bed-wetters with special physical problems?

Before you terminated training, did the bed-wetter toilet correctly on at least 50 percent of all his toileting opportunities and did he have no more than 1 accident?

Maintenance

Did the bed stay dry 7 consecutive nights before you terminated the use of the wet-bed alarm (Monitored Maintenance phase)?

After the Monitored Maintenance was terminated, did you always check the bed each morning and require Cleanliness Training if it was wet or praise if it was dry?

Was the bed-wetter's breakfast or other activity always delayed until he had completed Cleanliness Training?

Was a specific certified staff member assigned as Maintenance Supervisor on each working shift?

Did the entire ward staff take turns in serving as the Maintenance Supervisor?

	Not Sure	Definitely Not	Not Completely	Definitely Yes
Maintenance, cont.				
Was certification as a Maintenance Supervisor always postponed until a staff member demonstrated competency in conducting all facets of the Maintenance Program?	_____	_____	_____	_____
Did a second certified staff member serve as an Assistant Maintenance Supervisor on each shift?	_____	_____	_____	_____
Was each Nightly Maintenance Record sheet always filled in completely and accurately and initialed by the appropriate Maintenance Supervisor and conspicuously posted?	_____	_____	_____	_____
Was the Monthly Nighttime Accident Chart filled out correctly each night?	_____	_____	_____	_____
Institutional and Staff Support				
Did the Ward Supervisor or someone in a position of authority take responsibility for the toilet training program?	_____	_____	_____	_____
Did you obtain the active cooperation and continued support of the Institutional Director?	_____	_____	_____	_____
Did you provide the Institutional Director and other supervisors with a monthly progress report of the training results?	_____	_____	_____	_____
Did you discuss the training program with the entire staff prior to instituting the program and convince all of them of the need for the program?	_____	_____	_____	_____
Did you observe each Maintenance Supervisor's actual performance during the Maintenance Program?	_____	_____	_____	_____

REFERENCES

Ayllon, T., and N. H. Azrin. *The Token Economy: A Motivational System for Therapy and Rehabilitation.* New York, Appleton-Century-Crofts, 1968.

Azrin, N. H., C. Bugle, and F. O'Brien. "Behavioral Engineering: Two Apparatuses for Toilet Training Retarded Children," *Journal of Applied Behavior Analysis,* 1971, 4:249-253.

Azrin, N. H., and R. M. Foxx. "A Rapid Method of Toilet Training the Institutionalized Retarded," *Journal of Applied Behavior Analysis,* 1971, 4:89-99.

Azrin, N. H., R. M. Foxx, and F. O'Brien. "Toilet Training the Profoundly and Severely Retarded," *The Journal of Research and Training,* 1973, 1 (in press).

Azrin, N. H., S. J. Kaplan, and R. M. Foxx. "Autism Reversal: Eliminating Stereotyped Self-Stimulation of the Retarded," *American Journal of Mental Deficiency,* 1973, 78:241-248.

Azrin, N. H., T. J. Sneed, and R. M. Foxx. "Dry Bed: A Procedure for Eliminating Bed Wetting by the Retarded," *Behaviour Research and Therapy,* 1973, 11:427-434.

Bensberg, G. J. *Teaching the Mentally Retarded: A Handbook for Ward Personnel.* Atlanta, Southern Regional Education Board, 1965.

Foxx, R. M., and N. H. Azrin. "Restitution: A Method of Eliminating Aggressive-Disruptive Behavior of Retarded and Brain Damaged Patients, *Behaviour Research and Therapy,* 1972, 10:15-27.

_____. "The Elimination of Autistic Self-Stimulatory Behavior by Overcorrection," *Journal of Applied Behavior Analysis,* 1973, 6:1-14.

_____. "Dry Pants: A Rapid Method of Toilet Training Children," *Behaviour Research and Therapy,* 1973, 11:435-442.

Foxx, R. M., and P. L. Martin. "A Reliable Portable Timer," *Journal of Applied Behavior Analysis,* 1971, 4:60.

Webster, D. R., and N. H. Azrin. "Required Relaxation: A Method of Inhibiting Agitative-Disruptive Behaviors of Retardates," *Behaviour Research and Therapy,* 1973, 11:67-68.

NOTES ON THE TOILET TRAINING APPARATUSES

Since the publication of this book in 1973, most of the toilet training apparatuses used in this program no longer are being manufactured. However, the toilet training procedures can still be implemented without these apparatuses. For toilet training with individual clients, follow the procedures for home training discussed on page 96. For group training, blue litmus paper can be substituted for the urine alert and pants alarm as discussed on page 31. The wet-bed alarm currently is available from J.C. Penney.

INDEX

Accidents, daytime, after training, 74-75; while arising from toilet, 64; during bladder training, 48-49; caused by restrictive clothing, 85; daily record of, during Maintenance, 78-79; detection of, 31-33; dry-pants inspection procedure for, 46; at end of training day, 49-50; Full Cleanliness Training for, 55-57; hard-to-detect, 84-85; during home training, 96; intentional, 81; during Maintenance Program, 74-75, 79-87; during mealtimes or programmed activities, 81; due to misdirected urination, 64; monthly record of, 79-80; normal ward reaction to, 86-87; off-ward, 85; Positive Practice for, during bladder training, 48-49; Positive Practice for, during self-initiation training and Maintenance, 57, 74-75; pre-training record of, 25-27; resistance to cleaning up, 57-59; unavoidable, 85-86; while walking to or from toilet, 63. *See also* Bladder training

Accidents, nighttime. *See* Bed-Wetting

Administrative support, 89-93; 127-128

Administrators. *See* Toilet Training Co-ordinator; Institutional Director

Age to begin training, 24

Aggression, 59, 65-66

Allergies, 25

Ambulation, 23, 68-70. *See also* Non-ambulation

Apparatus, ordering information, 135. *See also* Pants alarm, Urine alert, Wet-bed alarm

Attendants. *See* Institutional staff

Bathroom, 27-29

Bed-Ridden. *See* Nonambulation

Bed-Wetting, detection of, 111; disapproval for, 113-115; in the elderly, 109-110; institutional factors in, 121-128; Maintenance Program for, 117-119, 123-128; Maintenance Supervisor for, 123; Monitored Mainenance for, 117-118, 123-126; monthly record of, 125-126; Nighttime Cleanliness Training for, 113-115; normal reaction to, 119; Positive Practice for, 113-115; pre-training record of, 121-122; prevalence of, 107-108; roaming at night and, 126; time required to eliminate, 110; trainables for program to eliminate, 109-110; trainers to eliminate, 121; training strategy to eliminate, 108-109; unavoidable, 118; urinating on floor and, 126; *vs.* daytime wetting, 107

Behavior modification, 19-20

Behavior problem, aggressiveness as a, 59, 65-66; resistiveness as a, 57-59; temper tantrums as a, 65-66; "testing" as a, 82

Bladder development, 20-21, 50, 109-110

Bladder training, accidents during, *see* Accidents, daytime; for the blind, 69-70; bowel control in, 50-51; Brief Cleanliness Training in, 48-49; candy and treats during, 33; checklist used for, 62; for children at home, 96-97; clothing for, 32-33; dressing skills for, 32-33, 41-44; dry-pants inspections in, 46, *see also* Dry-pants inspections; for the elderly, 95-96; flow chart of, 47; fluids used during, 34; flushing, toilet in, 44; graduated guidance in, 35-38; lack of self-initiation in, 67-68, *see also* Self-Initiation; lunch as a reward in, 47; Maintenance Program in, *see* same; materials required for, 28-29; medical examination before, 25; for the mentally ill, 95; misdirected urination during, 64; for the nonambulatory, 69-70; overview of, 35; physical requirements for, 23-24;

Geriatric patient, bed-wetting by, 109-110; daytime training for, 95-96; unsteady locomotion and, 68. See also Age

Gestures. See Prompts

Graduated guidance, 35-40; with bed-wetters, 114; with deaf, 69; as related to dressing skills, 41-44; in Full Cleanliness Training, 57, 83; with hyperactive residents, 65; Positive Practice and, 49, 57, 114; with resistive behavior, 50, 58-59; with temper tantrums, 65-66. See also Fading Guidance. See Graduated guidance

Habit training, 19. See also Bladder training

Home training, daytime, 96-97; nighttime, 107-119

Hyperactivity, 64-65

Imitation, learning by, 22,28

Incontinence, effects of, on residents, staff, and institution, 19, 89-90; institutional practices to eliminate, 89-91

Independent toileting. See Self-Initiation

Institutional Director, 89-92, 127-128

Institutional staff, ensuring cooperation and support of, 92-93; as daytime Maintenance Supervisors, 75-77; as nighttime Maintenance Supervisors, 123; as nighttime trainers, 121; supervision and motivation of, 23

Instructions. See Prompts

Intelligence. See IQ

IQ, easiest trained retardates and, 23, 28; prompt-fading technique and, 38; retardation classification by, 17; teaching a skill and, 35-36

Kidney function test, 25

Learning. See Motivation

Litmus paper, 31, 96

Lunch, 47

Maintenance Program, daytime, 71-93. See also Accidents, daytime; Dry-pants inspections; Full Cleanliness Training; Maintenance Supervisor; Monthly Accident Chart; Number of trainees; Positive Practice; Recording; Self-Initiation; Termination of

Maintenance Program

Maintenance Program, Monitored, 117-118, 123-126

Maintenance Program, nighttime, 117-119, 123-126. See also Bed-Wetting, Monthly Accident Chart, Nighttime Cleanliness Training, Number of trainees, Positive Practice, Recording, Maintenance Supervisor, Termination of Maintenance Program, Wet-bed alarm

Maintenance Supervisor, daytime, 75-77; nighttime, 123-125; non-Maintenance duties of, 77, 123

Males, clothing worn by, during daytime training, 32-33; misdirected urination by, 64; restrictive clothing worn by, 85

Manual guidance, 36. See also Graduated guidance

Masturbation, 66

Materials required for training, during daytime, 28-29; in home, 96-97; at night, 111-112

Mealtimes, failure to delay, 83; use in dry-pants inspections, 47, 71-75. See also Lunch

Medical examination, 25

Mentally ill, 95

Moisture-detecting snaps, 31-33

Monthly Accident Chart, daytime, 79-80; nighttime, 125-126

Monthly Training Summary, daytime, 90-92; nighttime, 127-128

Mopping. See Full Cleanliness Training

Motivation, 20-23

Motor skills, 23-24, 68-70

Neurological impairment. See Brain damage

Nighttime Cleanliness Training, 113-115

Nonambulation, 69-70, 96

Non-Maintenance Duties. See Maintenance Supervisor

Number of trainees, in daytime training, 27; in daytime Maintenance Program, 78; in nighttime Maintenance Program, 123

Number of trainers, 27, 56, 121

Pants alarm, 31-33, 44, 48, 62, 96

Parents. See Home training

Patient. See Number of trainees, Num-

Underpants, 27, 31-33
Untrainables, 17-19
Urinating on floor, 126
Urine alert, in bladder training, 29, 44, 62; for detecting appropriate eliminations, 29-31; in flushing toilet, 44; in home training, 96-97; in nighttime training, 110-112, 116

Wet. *See* Accidents, daytime; Bed-Wetting
Wet-bed alarm, 111-119, 122-123
Wheelchair. *See* Nonambulation